DALLAS PUBLIC AND PRIVATE

Books by Warren Leslie

THE BEST THING THAT EVER HAPPENED
LOVE OR WHATEVER IT IS
DALLAS PUBLIC AND PRIVATE

GROSSMAN PUBLISHERS · NEW YORK · 1964

DALLAS
public and private
WARREN LESLIE
ASPECTS OF AN AMERICAN CITY

Second Printing , March 1964

For Bonnie, who had the courage, with my love

Contents

The unexamined life is not worth living.

SOCRATES

DALLAS PUBLIC AND PRIVATE

1 | Introduction

In Dallas, the Club Imperial of the Baker Hotel is among the fashionable places in which to lunch. Its walls have a look of the inside of a sea shell, giving the place a quietly glistening effect that is not displeasing. The whole atmosphere is quiet; even at night, when a combo plays for dancing, the music is so discreet it is barely audible. Not many people come at night. The club was founded by Fenton Baker, when he owned the hotel, for his friends and theirs. He was a middle-aged man at the time, and this is not a young persons' club. Its membership is rich and influential, and it is one of the few clubs in town whose members may not issue a guest card to another Dallas resident. The club realizes that its members are human beings with human weaknesses —such as unsuitable friends. It simply wishes to protect the other members against these weaknesses.

On any weekday the room begins to fill at noon. Dallas is an early lunching city. At the Colony in New York the waiters have barely arrived by twelve, but at the Imperial in Dallas the customers are having their first martini by that time. At two the room will be almost empty. A couple of well-dressed women will linger over coffee, discussing their own or other people's divorces, and in the bar towards the rear a table of young bucks, full of second-generation money and empty hours, will order stingers on the rocks. But, if there is serious drinking to be done, the party will move elsewhere. Fenton Baker has been retired for some years now, but his stern shadow still dominates the Imperial. One simply did not drink too much at lunch in front of or within blocks of Mr. Baker, a man who did not even allow his bellboys to say good morning to him.

In a way, the Imperial tells a part of the Dallas story.

For many years it was not the Imperial at all. It was the Mural Room, it was open to the public, and it was the night club where a generation of Dallas people met, courted and danced to some of the best dance music in America. Along with these young Dallas people came outsiders: conventioneers, traveling salesmen, visiting lecturers and dress designers, out-of-town bankers, lawyers, doctors, newspapermen and motion picture people. Because of the peculiar Texas liquor laws, they brought their own bottles and drank too much rather than carry the bottle home. They bought set-ups and food; in those days few people drank wine. The hotel made money on the set-ups, lost money on the food, and had to close at midnight on weekdays and one o'clock on Saturdays because of the Texas curfew, a wartime measure that somehow lingers on. On such a schedule all night clubs must lose money, and the Mural Room lost a fortune each year. Following a trend, Mr. Baker closed his public room and turned it into a private club from which the general public is barred, including all out-of-towners —except those few who know someone in Dallas who is a member.

In this minor way and in many major ways, The Establishment of the city retreated a step further into its privacy, out of the reach of extraneous minds and tongues. And they meet each day at the Imperial or one of six or eight similar places to have a mixed drink (legal in private clubs) and to agree on things. The club now turns a handsome profit.

On November 22, 1963, I walked into the Imperial for lunch and a business discussion with Dr. Paul A. Goldschmidt, executive secretary of the United States–Austrian Chamber of Commerce in New York. It was a clear, cool day, and we were in good spirits. We had come from watching, with 200,000 others, a robust young President and his lovely wife motor slowly down Main Street on the way to his appointment at the Dallas Trade Mart. We were impressed, as was the President, by the great warmth and good will which emanated from the huge crowd in this anti-Administration city, though Goldschmidt did remark that he was surprised that there were no ropes to hold people away from the President's open car, and that Main Street had not been blocked off for the occasion. As the Presidential motorcade proceeded west, eastbound traffic continued normally, halted only momentarily as the motorcade passed.

No more than ten minutes after our arrival at the club, the phone rang for me. It was brought to the table.

My secretary said, "There's this awful rumor the President's been shot. We can't get anybody—newspapers, radio stations—on the phone. Turn on the television."

Goldschmidt, watching my face change, grabbed my arm. "My God, what is it?" he said.

Before I could speak, a short, square man with a ruddy face burst into the club like a lunatic.

"Turn on the television," he yelled. "The President's shot!"

A waiter turned it on. A face first, then its voice: "All we know," it said, "is that President Kennedy and Governor Connally *have* been shot . . ."

In back of me, a man threw his head down on his arm against the table.

"This God-damned town," he said quietly.

In the silence that followed, the wheeze in one man's breathing sounded thunderous against the voice of the announcer. When it was announced that the President was dead, chairs were pushed back, drinks and lunches left untouched, and men left in silence to close their offices. Later, unwilling to face their homes, some came back and watched television until the club itself closed at six. Then we all went home, beginning that long, terrible weekend, the silence of which was shattered by a single pistol shot in the Dallas jail.

What follows is not the story of an assassination. It is the story of a city. The story should have been written long before the President came to Dallas, but it wasn't.

The assassination itself, the demented act of a human outcast, is no part of this story. Instead, I wish to write about a city which was not the inevitable site for a Presidential murder, but which *was* a logical place for something unpleasant and embarrassing to happen. So logical that Ambassador Adlai Stevenson almost advised the President to cancel his trip. So logical that a group of leading citizens nearly warned the President not to visit their own town. So logical that the town's efforts to avoid an incident were monumental; thinking people half expected something to happen. So logical that the shock and horror of the first hours were reactions to the enormity of the act, not because a violent act of some sort had taken place.

It is an extraordinary thing when an American city does not trust itself to receive the President of the United States in dignity. Dallas did not so trust itself—and with reason. This book is an attempt to show why. If it is a Texas story, it is also an American story. To place a local guilt and exonerate the rest of our country is as naive as some of the people of Dallas have themselves been during the years when the storm clouds were banking. The forces of violence exist everywhere. Unchallenged, unrepudiated, they grow and fester, gaining in confidence, attracting new strength.

The assassination focused the world's attention on Dallas and its dreary history of political extremism and violence. I write in the hope that the general implications of these particulars will be obvious and I write in the strange mixture of love and pain which many people of Dallas feel today. For this city, not nearly so black as the world press has painted it, was nevertheless not innocent in these matters. It was not innocent.

The world has indeed treated Dallas and Texas harshly. "Do not bring your children to this city" was the lead paragraph of a news story in Lord Beaverbrook's *London Evening Standard,* written by his granddaughter. "Giants 27, Assassins 21," somebody said, and it was a shock to understand that the "Assassins" were the Cowboys, Dallas' professional football team.

"Where you living now?" a bartender at the St. Regis in New York asked an old customer, a former New Yorker.

"Still in Dallas."

"I'd have thought you'd be coming home by now," the bartender said. "Or going somewhere."

In Los Angeles, shortly after the assassination, a fashion writer for the *Dallas News,* covering the California market, found it impossible to get room service. "Seems to take a little longer for the people from Dallas," a waiter explained.

In New York, a returning visitor to Europe spent less

time than usual in customs. "Dallas," the customs official said, looking at her declaration. "Hell, don't stick around here. Just go on home." He walked away.

After studying the city for a short time, a visiting journalist said, "If I were a liberal living in Dallas, I might feel I had to shoot a President just to get attention."

And a familiar remark now, among the thousands that have been made about the Dallas police: "I don't think the Dallas police force is so bad—look how quickly they caught Ruby."

The citizen of Dallas, traveling after the assassination, has also heard many expressions of sympathy. In some ways, the sympathy is more humiliating than the scorn. It seems to make of the city something special, even unique, and, by extension, it makes curiosities of its residents. Many people have asked me to explain to them certain aspects of the city, and I have tried, sitting up until the small hours. I wonder whether I have really succeeded in making them understand. So many words have been written and so much anger and sorrow has risen up against Dallas that even thoughtful people have a tendency to think in headlines, to grasp half a truth, and to understand a distortion.

On the other hand, some of the city's leaders, fighting back, have fought also with half-truths and distortions.

They have fought an emotional, predictable reaction, resulting from the death in Dallas of a young President, better loved, perhaps, than he knew. They have not faced up to more reflective criticism, which has posed questions such as:

Why were there three murders in Dallas that weekend, instead of one? Weren't two of these murders preventable?

Why was Ambassador Adlai Stevenson struck and spat upon in Dallas? Why was Lyndon Johnson nearly mobbed?

Why did Major General Walker choose Dallas in which to live?

Why did Dallas have to take such elaborate precautions to insure President Kennedy a welcome normal to any President of the United States?

Why did the *Dallas News* run a right-wing extremist advertisement on the day Kennedy arrived?

Why do so many Dallas leaders keep saying, "It was not our fault. It could have happened anywhere. Dallas is a great city"?

Is Dallas a part of the United States? Or is it some savage country of its own?

Dallas is indeed a part of the United States, but there are many, including a good many Texans, who believe that the city has become disturbed psychologically and confused morally, and that while such difficulties are scarcely unique in Dallas, they have been underlined there because of local factors which *are* unique. One such critic is Professor Reese McGee, head of the sociology department at the University of Texas. Writing in *The Nation* shortly after the assassination, Professor McGee said, "Barring the probability of Mississippi, in a doomed and fated way it had to be Texas and, in Texas, Dallas."

The reasons he stated were: (1) the absolutist nature of local thought; (2) the institutionalization of personalized violence; (3) the proliferation of firearms and the habit of carrying them; (4) the political respectability of the radical right; and (5) the nonexistence, publicly, of a radical left.

(Of the several thousand people I have met in Texas, I know almost none who carry firearms. Professor McGee's other points seem to me sound.)

After the November events, several meetings were held throughout Dallas to consider what action, if any, the city should take. Sometimes discussion revolved around what kind of memorial would be fitting as a tribute from Dallas to the memory of the late President. But at a few of these meetings the participants tried hard to get to the roots of the city's problems, and for one gathering, Dr. Robert E. Stoltz, chairman of the department of psychology at Southern Methodist University, prepared a professional report on aspects of Dallas.

Although at the time it was confidential and was not released to the press, it is quoted here with Dr. Stoltz's permission. It may have had more impact than the psychologist had foreseen, for it gave professional validity to the uneasiness many Dallas people had felt about their city.

It is my professional opinion [Dr. Stoltz wrote] that the current situation in Dallas could be described as follows:

A. There are elements in the city that encourage irresponsibility in the conduct of civic, political and personal affairs. The best organized and most vocal are the extreme right-wing groups. Evidence would suggest that they are also the most numerous and best financed. This condition is by no means unique. It can be found throughout the country, but the influence of these groups is greater here than in most cities. . . .

  (1) Violence as a means of settling disputes is accepted and condoned in our community. This is a practice of long standing in our nation but is particularly strong in this area and throughout the South. As evidence, note our homicide rate, which is about the eighth highest in the nation. While some groups may not direct acts of violence or lead them, it is to be expected that irresponsible words can lead to irresponsible

actions and that violence is very likely to characterize some of these acts. Witness our public behavior during and following the Alger-Johnson incident.

(2) To date there has been no organized and vocal opposition to these groups. There is no effective liberal group that exists to counter the thrust from the right. Lack of local opposition to a particular group's point of view is likely to encourage the group [in thinking] that this is the only correct view. They will have few doubts and they will repress the rest of the community. A clash of views often leads to new solutions, sometimes more creative ones. . . .

(3) In such groups, without restraints on what is required in the way of evidence and logic, there is a tendency of each member to try to exceed the other in attracting attention and in controlling. There is no *upper* limit to the kinds of charges or attacks that can be made.

(4) In the absence of any organized opposition to these groups, it is to be expected that individual citizens with less education, less self-control, or less stability could get the impression that certain actions would be desired and supported by the general community. It is quite likely that a great many of these actions would have violent out-

comes. Witness the mob action that can occur when public leaders take either no stand or support a stand with regard to aggressive action, i.e., the current situation in the deep South. As a contrast consider the success of the Dallas effort to integrate peaceably.

B. Leadership of Dallas has given lip service to humane and moral values, but has shown that it values the physical and economic aspects of the community primarily. Obviously there are a few exceptions. . . . A strong emphasis on materialism is evident in this community.

(1) Dallas has tended to define "goodness" in physical terms, such as the size and number of churches, length, breadth and height of buildings and expressways and the low frequency of incidents of corruption and vice. It ignores other statistics of "goodness" which are available but less flattering —homicide rates, vehicular deaths, poverty, medical care for some types of patients, quality of education, evidences of real culture, etc.

(2) The citizens of Dallas are beginning to associate any claim of doing something for the public good with latent and hidden economic gains for the sponsors of some mysterious group known as "they." It should be no surprise that many citizens develop a "what-is-in-it-for-me?" attitude

when they feel it is the philosophy of their leaders. Again, there are exceptions, but they are hard to find.

(3) Many leaders of Dallas have taken positions suggesting that they view men as by nature evil, and controllable only by economic forces rather than by appeals to reason or moral principle. Witness the recent pleas for a pay raise for police officers in order to "keep them from becoming corrupt." It is difficult to know the moral effect of views such as this on the police department at large. Obviously, it cannot be positive.

C. The lines of communication in the city are inadequate and the leadership is sharply stratified. We are developing a climate in which groups do not experience a mutual exchange of views and situations where rational and reasonable evaluation of facts and hypotheses is impossible. We have a large number of one-sided debates going on in which each group hears only its prior views, with slight additions and no contradictions. The newspapers in our community have contributed heavily to this condition. . . .

D. Dallas today is frustrated. It would like to escape blame and all its responsibilities. . . . But it finds that this is difficult. It would like to believe that these events could have happened anywhere, but it is having trouble convincing even itself. Everyone remembers the string of incidents preceding this one and our all too obvious effort to control incidents on the day of the assassination. I would agree that this is not the only place where this could have happened. But it is one of the places where it or something like it was quite likely to happen. . . .

E. In a situation such as this, the citizens will attempt to do one of several things to escape the feeling of guilt and frustration:

(1) Deny any responsibility for the events of [November 22-4]. Some will emphasize that this could have happened anywhere and see no association between the events of preceding weeks and these.

(2) Seek a scapegoat. . . . [which] will have the following characteristics: Be easy to identify, have lower status and less power than the groups seeking the scapegoats. Likely scapegoats are political leaders, police officials, foreign elements, minority groups. A typical approach would be to point out the deficiencies of other cities.

(3) Some will make an effort to atone for guilt in a physical way. One approach would be the naming of a street for the deceased, giving money, erecting a physical memorial. In short, in a way which will look like a costly change but which will avoid real change within themselves.

F. Any group attempting to enter into a power

vacuum and to enlist the aid and support of the community will have to do the following:

(1) It will speak with the appearance of authority. It will be helpful if such "authority" has the support of an organization which appears to have substantial following already.

(2) It will appear to have the support of the community. Certainly it will appear to have the support of some known community power figures.

(3) An important aspect of its program will be that it will appear to have a moral and/or patriotic basis of foundation.

(4) It will have a way of communicating with the community that will be of a continuing nature. It will either be aided by the mass media or it will develop a way of keeping in touch with the community through its own publications or spokesman. It may do both.

(5) It will have a central theme which is very simple in its construction, phraseology and conceptual level. It will not promote complex ideologies or concepts at first.

(6) It will sponsor and encourage a program of action. The first actions will be specific, again simple, and probably involve some physical involvement by the individuals.

(7) To encourage support, it will urge that the individual make some sort of public com-

mitment of agreement with the beliefs and purposes of the organization. This may be as simple as signing a membership card or as complex as undergoing elaborate initiation proceedings.

(8) It will develop a distinctive symbol or label so that a member can be immediately recognized both by other members and by the public.

(9) It will be quick to attach negative labels to those who are non-members.

(10) In its formative stages, it will avoid ambiguity or vagueness. It will not accept inactivity. Complex planning and sluggish inactivity will be avoided.

G. The groups that appear to meet these criteria most closely are the right-wing extremist groups. It is not unlikely that they could benefit most from the present situation. Competing groups are either nonexistent at present or, judging from their leadership and past behavior, will do nothing and wait a return to "normal." Current efforts by some persons in the community, notably religious leaders, are likely to fail because of lack of organization, limited total community involvement, or because their appeals are too vague, involve no specific direct action or because they have no ability to coordinate their efforts. For example, the Dallas Citizens' Council does not extend far into the community, is likely to delay action, does not have a fundamentally moral base and has little internal unity with regard to the task at hand. . . .

H. Studies of previous similar situations indicate that unless some efforts toward change occur, the problems we now have will continue to be with us and are very likely to increase. This is not over yet. It can get worse.

2 | Five cities in the middle of nowhere

For anyone who has a stake in Dallas, there is something touching about driving into town at sunset. Suddenly out of the flatness of the land a skyline appears, and it is a decent metropolitan skyline, though perhaps not one of the world's beauty marks. Since the air is normally clear in this arid country, the colors of the sunset are Matisse colors; rounding a bend in the road or topping a hill, one blinks in surprise at the boldness of the vision. Much of the essence of Dallas is in this skyline. The towers that stretch up belong to the great insurance companies, Southland Life, Fidelity Union Life and others, and to the banks, Republic, First National and Mercantile, with a couple of big hotels and some general office buildings around them. These days it is hard to see Magnolia's Flying Red Horse, which once topped the tallest building in town. An Englishman, Sir Alfred Bossom, built the Magnolia in 1922, and it was the pride of Dallas. Today, it is a low-flying horse, dwarfed by the deadly competition between the banks and insurance companies, the symbols of money, to show physically their size and power, to indicate unmistakably to the stranger that they run things in Dallas.

If the citizen of Dallas is moved by his skyline, it is less from aesthetics than from a sense of pride that it exists at all. The truth is, there really isn't any reason for Dallas. It sits in the middle of nowhere and nothing. The land around it is dry, black and unproductive; farmers do battle with it to exist. The only natural waterway is the Trinity River which is, alternately, almost invisible or flooding to the danger point. To call it a river at all is a sample of native Dallas overstatement. One hundred and twenty-three years ago, when the city was founded, the nearest railroad was hundreds of miles away. The oil derrick is unknown in Dallas and no gas, no sulphur have ever been found there.

Yet in certain ways it is the most powerful city in a powerful state. It is the largest inland city in the nation, and it continues to grow. Without important natural advantages, it is an improbable city, as man-made as the lakes around it; it is the creation of the citizens. It has not been pushed in any given direction by circumstances it could not avoid. Whatever it is did not come about because of the presence of the sea, a major river, the railroad, oil or a major industry.

Instead, it has been shaped as few cities have ever been by *men,* and much of the psychology of Dallas traces back to this. And men, taking the credit for what the city is, must also take the responsibility for what it is not.

Its existence is an invention of the human mind and a tribute to human energy. For *Fortune* magazine in 1949, Holland McCombs wrote: "Properly it should never have become a city . . . yet there Dallas stands—its skyscrapers soaring abruptly up from the black land like Maxfield Parrish castles and so wildly, improbably successful. Yet the stranger leaves it feeling as if he had been suspended in a vast hyperbole. It is the Athens of the Southwest, the undisputed leader of finance, insurance, distribution, culture and fashion for this land of the super-Americans. And now it is becoming a great manufacturing center as well. It is one of the cleanest, best policed, best managed cities in the country and one of the fastest growing—from 377,000 people in 1940 to almost a half a million today. [And nearly a million in 1963.] Everything in Dallas is bigger and better; the parties are plushier, the buildings are more air-conditioned, the women better dressed and the girls more fetching. And in all of these things, it is finally a monument to sheer determination. Dallas doesn't owe a thing to accident, nature or inevitability. It is what it is—even to the girls—because the men of Dallas damn well planned it that way."

The men McCombs was writing about were and are exclusively businessmen. What they have done has been business-directed and what they have done successfully puts other American drummers and Babbitts to shame. Back in the 1870s, Dallas had a population of less than 4,000 and clearly wasn't going to get much bigger unless it could get the railroad to come through.

The Houston & Texas Central Railroad was planning to by-pass Dallas on its way north from Corsicana. As a matter of fact, the railroad scarcely knew there was a town named Dallas. But some determined citizens raised $5,000 and gave it with 115 acres of land and several miles of free right-of-way to the H&TC. Absolutely amazed, the railroad did a little bending around and managed to hit Dallas on its way north. The case was a little different with the Texas & Pacific, which was not interested in cash or land. So some men of Dallas paid a visit to the state legislature at Austin and managed to persuade the legislature to attach a codicil to the T&P's right-of-way bill. You had to look three or four times to find it but, sure enough, the bill specified that trains would have to stop within a mile of a watering spot called Browder Springs. Browder Springs was in Dallas; so, to its surprise, was the T&P.

Always the merchants, the bankers and later the utility men have led the way. In 1936, Texas celebrated its centennial—one hundred years of some of America's most fascinating history. The big celebration took place in Dallas in spite of the fact that Dallas had less reason to be the site than any other major city of the state. No treaty has ever been signed in Dallas, no battles have been fought there, and about the only historical relic in the area is the log cabin John Neely Bryan lived in when he settled the city. Even today, sightseeing tours of Dallas for convention groups and other visitors are severely limited by the fact that there are not many sights to see.

Nevertheless, Dallas sent a delegation to Austin in 1936. It had $3,500,000 in hand, an energy and determination that awed the legislators, and an entertainment program that may have hospitalized some of them.

Predictably the Texas Centennial, taking the form of a great fair, came to Dallas and gave the city its national image as the most important in Texas.

Dallas is not what the visitor to Texas expects. In fact, it has been called "the best northern city in the South." Its citizens like to compare it with New York and San Francisco rather than with other Texas cities, and there is a point in these comparisons. Fort Worth, for example, still has a very western flavor. It calls itself the place "Where the West Begins," and one still sees the big hats and hears the cowboy drawl on the streets of Fort Worth. Houston has a wheeling and dealing, shoot-from-the-hip atmosphere in which every man is on his own and a little flamboyance is neither unexpected nor unwelcome. San Antonio, with its roots deep in Texas history and a large Spanish-speaking population, has the charm of an older world about it.

Dallas is a business city, especially a financial center, and its dollar power allies it closely with Wall Street. Its people have faith that they are culturally ahead of other Texas cities, that its women are much better dressed and that it is, indeed, "the Athens of the Alfalfa Fields," which it used to be called. Most of these images are open to doubt these days, but they are deeply held. The newspapers still compare the Dallas summer musicals to Broadway, the Dallas Civic Opera to the Metropolitan, and the Dallas Symphony Orchestra to the New York Philharmonic.

Dallas today is five cities, or at least five quite dissimilar population bodies; so dissimilar that there are five Browning Societies within the city limits, all dedicated to the study of the poets and their work but divided both in terms of geography and economic strata. The sociologist could divide Dallas up more precisely and would end with ten, twelve or more such areas but, for these purposes, five will be sufficient. While they are different, they are all part of the city itself, and looking at each of them gives insight into the personality and character of Dallas.

Oak Cliff lies west of the center of town. From downtown one goes west as far as possible, turning left or right at the Post Office Terminal Building. Going left, one passes Dealey Plaza and the handsome *Dallas News* Building with its adjoining television station, and drives over the Houston Street Viaduct, crossing the Trinity River, on into Oak Cliff. Going right at the Post Office Building, one turns left to a triple underpass and continues into Oak Cliff by way of the Fort Worth cut-off. The triple underpass marks the end of downtown Dallas to the west. It is the landmark President Kennedy never reached in safety. On the northwest corner of the intersection of Elm and Houston streets stands the Texas Book Depository. A generation of Dallas people, reaching this point, have wondered openly which of three buildings standing together might be the ugliest: the Book Depository, the Records Building which is adjacent to it and contains the county jail, or the old Texas Gothic Courthouse where sit the county judge and commissioners. It is ironic and bitter to many Dallas citizens that of three murders committed during the weekend of November 22, one was done no more than thirty yards from the county jail and the other was done *in* the city jail.

Stretching out from the viaduct or the underpass is the community of Oak Cliff. It is part of the city of Dallas and all of its government comes from Dallas. Two hundred and seventy-five thousand people live there. In the older parts of the community which are the ones closest to downtown, the houses are mainly small, old and dingy, and so are the apartments. Out further, in tribute to industrial growth in the area between Dallas and Fort Worth, the houses and apartments are fresh and new. Parts of the old section of Oak Cliff are naturally prettier than anything in North Dallas. Down through Colorado Boulevard into Kessler Park, one finds a few of those Dallas rarities, hills and woods. Out further, the Oak Cliff Country Club has one of the most scenic settings in the city. It is much easier to get downtown from Oak Cliff than from North Dallas, and most Oak Cliff people work in Dallas. But many of them are employed in the warehouses of the Great Southwest Industrial District between Dallas and Fort Worth and thousands of others at Ling-Temco-Vought's Grand Prairie facilities.

In spite of its natural beauty, Oak Cliff is unfashionable. A young man coming to Dallas with his family and anxious to get ahead downtown may well begin his life in Oak Cliff because he can find a house at a good price in a pleasant setting, close to his work. But unless his business is intimately connected with Oak Cliff, he may soon move out of the area and into North Dallas, where he will pay more for the same house, which will be farther from his office and will lie, usually, on a flat plot of ground surrounded by other houses just like his. He will explain that he has done this because most of his friends live north of town. The actual reason is that he has found that by living in Oak Cliff he and his wife are out of the mainstream of Dallas life and that his children will grow up out of this mainstream.

For example, very few Oak Cliff residents are directors or sponsors of the Dallas Symphony Orchestra, and just as few Oak Cliff women are members of the Dallas Civic Opera Guild. Before the Contemporary Arts Museum merged with the Dallas Museum of Fine Arts, only a few Oak Cliff residents were on the membership rolls. In the prestige cultural organizations, in which membership counts greatly toward family image, Oak Cliff is almost invisible.

Every year, in their usual desperate hunt for money and support, these various organizations will hear somebody get up and say, "Why don't we get Oak Cliff in on this? It's their orchestra (opera, theater, whatever), as well as ours." Everyone nods wisely, but at the end of the year Oak Cliff remains sparsely represented. Psychologically, part of this is probably because Oak Cliff residents *feel* that they are unfashionable and that the chic citizens of North Dallas, though interested in Oak Cliff money, are not otherwise interested in them.

As a result, the sprawling community has turned inward on itself like a rejected child. Oak Cliff people bank in Oak Cliff and buy insurance from their neighbors. They buy cars in Oak Cliff. They buy most of their clothes, toys, household furnishings, refrigerators and everything else in Oak Cliff. They do all this at one of the big new shopping villages, or they buy from the old line Jefferson Avenue merchants who have for years commanded a loyalty which might well be the envy of some of the big downtown stores. About the only thing Oak Cliff people don't buy in Oak Cliff is liquor, beer or wine. They don't do that because they can't. In 1958, the precinct voted itself "dry." Texas is a local option state, and cities and precincts within a city can vote themselves "dry" or "wet." The vote, of course, has nothing to do with drinking habits. Because the community has grown, Oak Cliff citizens drink more than they did before they voted to be "dry." All the law means is that they must make their purchases before leaving downtown.

Although the election sent a dank chill into the hearts of other Dallas citizens who were afraid it might lead to the drying up of the whole town, it has not. Actually, the Oak Cliff vote was not surprising. The area has always prided itself on having more churches (215) than any other area of Dallas and more churches on one block (ten, on Tenth Street) than any other place in the world. The preaching is somewhat more fundamentalist than it is in the northern section of the city, and old-fashioned outdoor revival meetings, sometimes with faith healing, are still held in the shadow of Oak Cliff.

The beer and wine election sadly eliminated a bit of the color of Dallas. In the days when these refreshments could be sold legally, Oak Cliff was at once the church capital of the city and the sin capital of the city. Lined up and down the Fort Worth cut-off was a score of night clubs, some featuring the popular strippers of the day. Organized prostitution flourished in dozens of motels and most of the pimps of the city lived in Oak Cliff in order to keep a careful tab on the girls' tallies. It was a dull night when a couple of girls didn't get into a rip-roaring fight about something, or the police didn't find a cache of heroin in somebody's motel room, or somebody didn't knife somebody else in a barroom brawl, or some hoodlum was not shot by another for making eyes at the wrong girl.

Years ago, when I was still on the staff of the *Dallas News*, Houston passed a local ordinance limiting the amount of clothes a stripper could take off—or rather stating the amount of clothes she had to keep on. Tom Dillard, a photographer, and I were assigned to go out and do an interview with the Dallas delegation of striptease artists to get their comments.

Locating the girls was no problem; we simply drove out the cut-off and went from one motel to another. They flocked out to greet us like quail. For me it was an unusually amusing assignment, but for Dillard it could have been a career. One newspaper picture means a lot more to a stripper than some quotes on what she thinks about current events. Dillard was treated like a sultan; towards the end of the day he began to feel like one.

A good many of the livelier ladies of the community still live in Oak Cliff, but most of them have branched out now to other sections of the city. The night clubs are all gone and the Fort Worth cut-off is a jumble of auto lots, junk dealers and other eyesores. These days it is a wasteland unrelieved even by the healthy bustle of sin.

In the shadow of the downtown skyscrapers lie the slums, the second city of Dallas. One general area is called West Dallas. Close to Oak Cliff, it was not even a part of the city until recently. It was not annexed because the city fathers simply did not wish to face the huge problem of cleaning it up. Public and newspaper pressure finally brought about annexation, and the shacks and privies of West Dallas are now as definitely a part of the city as the million-dollar buildings downtown. Sightseeing visitors are not normally taken to West Dallas or South Dallas, areas of which are just as blighted.

Some years ago the English writer J. B. Priestley was in town, and I drove him around the better residential districts. "Very nice," he said. "Now I know how Neiman-Marcus customers live. Tell me, where do your elevator operators live?" We drove to the Hall Street Negro section and then into South Dallas. "And your white family of five earning $2,500 a year—where does it live?" We drove to West Dallas, trying to stick to the ten miles of paved streets and away from the thirty-three miles of dirt and gravel roads. We watched the dirty, ragged children playing stickball, and we passed the building where Brother Bill Harrod annually collects his donations of shoes so that these children can wear something on their feet.

"I think," Priestley said, "that you have a puncture in your balloon."

In 1949 I did a few stories about West Dallas as part of the *Dallas News'* annual campaign to get something done about the area. I don't remember all the families I interviewed, but I remember one of them well. Most of these people were obviously going to depend on some sort of charity all their lives: old people, illiterates and semi-literates and that inevitable small percentage of human beings who spend their lives scraping together enough money for another bottle of cheap wine.

The family I remember was headed by a woman. She was thirty years old and looked forty. She had eight children; the oldest was twelve and the youngest, a girl, less than a year. They lived in two rooms. There were three double beds, a couple of wooden chairs and no refrigerator; also, no water. They bought water from tank trucks at fifty cents a barrel. The bathroom was a box privy outside. I must have said something accusing about a husband who would desert his family. Sitting on one of the beds, she shook her head.

"No," she said, "you got um wrong. He wuz doin' us a favor. See, he ran an elevator an' even if that don't pay much, we wuz gettin' by. But then, they tore down the buildin', an' he got fired. See, Jack's like me. He ain't trained for nothin'. He never even got to high school, like me. He tried an' tried to find somethin'. Nobody needed um. So he went to try an' get some help, just for a while. Some agency, I dunno. Anyway, they told um he was okay—you know, not sick—an' they couldn't help um. The law says they couldn't. So he come back home, pretty low. One day, he cut out, just cut out. I tried to find um, but it's like he just disappeared—just gone, zip!

"So now, see, we can get nearly a hunnert a month 'cause he deserted us. An' I got a job in the laundry, pays about twenny a week. Kid nearby comes an' looks out for the little one when I'm gone. We couldn't have the hunnert a month if he was here. He wuz doin' us a favor, he thought.

"Only trouble is, he don't know how much we love um. We really love um. The kids, they ain't the same at all since he's gone. They don't mind me; they don't do nothin' that's right. But he thought he was doin' right. He knew the agency couldn't help us unless he cleared out. So he's gone, zip, just like that! An' I can't find um nowhere. Don't seem fair, somehow. See, we really love um. An' he loves us."

Since that talk in 1949, not a great deal has changed in West Dallas. Jack would still have to clear out or be physically disabled if his wife were to receive welfare aid. There would be no change in the house, unless by this time it has fallen down. The little girl would be fifteen now, and the chances are she is either married or soon will be, and that she will produce about the same litter as her mother and live in the same circumstances.

The slums of Dallas, like all slums, perpetuate themselves.

In 1963 roughly 45,000 people lived in West Dallas.
Figures show that in the whole city there are about
22,000 substandard family dwelling units and that about
75,000 to 85,000 people live in them. Three thousand
families have no piped water and in 8,000 homes there
is neither a bathtub nor a shower. The median income
for the people living in slum areas is less than $3,000 a
year. The reasons for such low income levels are the
usual ones: illiteracy, old age, sickness and abandon-
ment. In Dallas County more than 14,000 old people
are drawing the maximum $83 a month. The deserted
mother I knew would be drawing $107 a month. Some-
one totally disabled would draw $69 a month; someone
blind would draw $90.

One of the major problems in eliminating slums and
substandard housing is where you put the people now
living there. In 1963, Mayor Earle Cabell proposed that
3,000 public housing units be built in Dallas, half of
which would go to the city's aged and the other half
of which would go to the city's low-income Negroes. In
his mayoralty campaign, Cabell had promised to try to
do something about the Dallas slums and this was his
solution, or at least the first step in a solution. Cabell's
idea was simply that it would be nice if private enterprise could erect such low-cost housing, but that it

couldn't. He said time and again that he would be de-
lighted to receive a workable plan from private enterprise to solve the problem; since he had not received
such a plan, he felt the only alternative was public
housing largely supported by federal monies.

He was supported by the League of Women Voters,
which issued a statement through Mrs. John K. Godbey,
the president, that the league was supporting the may-
or's plan because "private enterprise cannot supply decent housing for these people at a price they can afford
to pay." The mayor was also backed by the *Dallas Morning News*.

But he was opposed by a determined group of realtors and builders for whom "public housing" is a term
that chills the heart as the term "socialized medicine"
does the hearts of doctors. The president of the Dallas
Real Estate Board, Lawrence Gallaway, admitted that
he hadn't the vaguest idea of what to do about providing housing for the indigent aged at $25 a month. "It's
doubtful in my mind that private industry can do it—
but let's start saying no to Washington," he said.

It is not that the public housing unit was presented to
Dallas as something new and shocking. The city already
has about 6,400 dwelling units, about 3,500 for Negroes,
600 for Mexicans and 2,200 for white people. For these
units the federal government puts up $25 per unit per
month to help low-income people pay the rent, or at

least the government will, when it is necessary. The Dallas Housing Authority actually has not used the maximum. In 1961 it accepted a subsidy of $21.91 per unit per month. Even before the mayor's proposal there was about $50,000,000 worth of public housing in the city.

Perhaps a politically wise mayor would not propose any solution to the slum problem but only deplore its existence every six months or so. This would indicate the mayor's social conscience without, at the same time, offending the vested interests of the builders and realtors. A Dallas mayor, I think, could be re-elected innumerable times without doing anything at all about the slums, so long as he mentioned them now and then.

Acting out of courage and humanity, Mayor Cabell may have made a political error in trying to get the slums rebuilt. His proposal of the 3,000 new units was characterized as "creeping socialism." His resulting challenge to private enterprise to offer some solution of its own brought about a rather complicated plan which was turned down by the Federal Housing Authority as impractical. Fighting hard, he went to the all-powerful Citizens' Council and asked them for help. Some of the members were for him and some of them were against him; when it was all over the Council didn't do anything at all. Eventually the matter reached the voters and Mayor Cabell was defeated by a vote of 39,000 to 25,000.

It was a tough defeat for him, but it was a lot tougher for somewhere between 75,000 and 100,000 people who were in effect told by the rest of the citizenry that they could stay where they were and like it. For Mayor Cabell the defeat will be especially punishing now that he has decided to run for Congress against Republican incumbent Bruce Alger. The mayor's espousal of public housing will give Alger the chance to call him a "socialist." Cabell's consolation is that Alger will also have to call the *Dallas Morning News* and the League of Women Voters "socialistic enterprises," a concept so hilarious that Alger might be wiser not to bring it up.

The slum problem is not hopeless. The Dallas Action Committee for Community Improvement is under the direction of Les Potter, head of the Lone Star Gas Company (and, incidentally, a resident of Oak Cliff). It has issued a couple of reports advising the city to clean up West Dallas within four years, using city bond funds for providing water, a sanitary sewer system and street paving extensions. The committee has also advised a firmer enforcement of housing codes and has recognized that the community as a whole must provide economic support for housing the low-income population. However, it specifically declined to speculate about "what should be the source or form of such public support." Obviously you can either increase public assistance grants or you can decrease the cost of housing, which means public housing. The committee did not recommend either one.

Out of its surveys, however, and out of the *Sturm und Drang* of the public housing controversy, some good things have happened. In 1963 the park department completed a recreation center in West Dallas which cost about $400,000—more money than has been spent in all the years heretofore on the area by the park department. The Dallas United Community Centers increased from four to six the number of recreation centers in West Dallas and more than doubled its annual budget from $50,000 to $110,000.

But as of the moment, five out of the eight children in the family I visited will drop out before they finish high school. One or two of them will end up outside the law and the others will buy their water at fifty cents a barrel, as their mother still does.

Sociologists tend to think of Dallas as a home-owning town, as a city where most social activity centers around the home. In many ways this is still true. Dallas people generally entertain more in their homes than they do in clubs and restaurants, partly because there aren't very many interesting clubs or restaurants. A new development over the last ten years, however, is that the "home" is likely to be an apartment.

Driving around the city these days, a visitor might

well think of Dallas as home-selling rather than home-owning. The FOR SALE signs are everywhere—on big houses, small houses and medium-sized houses. Many people, of course, are trading an older home for a newer one. Home building still continues, although it has leveled off in recent years. It isn't easy to sell an older house in Dallas these days; it is in competition with too many other older houses and with all the handsome new ones.

A great many people, however, are not trading one house for another, but rather a house for an apartment. Over the past two years, 21,000 apartment units costing $8,000,000 have been built in the Dallas area and at least 50,000 people live in them. Together, these people —plus an equal number who live in older buildings— comprise the third city of Dallas.

When an apartment rents for more than $250 a month, it is usually characterized as a luxury apartment and it will often be occupied by a childless couple, a single woman or a single man. In the higher bracketed apartments, say from $400 a month up, one often finds older couples, widows or widowers who have had large and expensive homes that were simply too much trouble to keep up after the children left. There are thousands of apartments like these and more going up all the time.

The newest luxury apartments are on Turtle Creek Boulevard. Turtle Creek, which actually begins The Es-

tablishment area by our definition, was once the pretti-
est residential street in the city of Dallas. The creek is an
honest-to-God creek. The trees on its banks are really
beautiful, and there are still some gracious old homes
down the boulevard and off into the surrounding streets.
One side of Turtle Creek, however, is disappearing for
the homes and the time may not be too far off when the
other side goes as well. One sees now a series of high-
rise apartment buildings such as 3525 Turtle Creek,
Turtle Creek North and others. There is even a big
health club called "the Spa" where the old woods used
to be.

If one is going to live in an apartment, any address
on Turtle Creek becomes the most fashionable one can
have. To live, for example, at 3525 Turtle Creek, which
was the first luxury, high-rise apartment building in the
area, is a status symbol that can work in two ways. If
one is a member of The Establishment, even if retired,
or if one wishes to be a member of The Establishment,
3525 is a satisfactory address.

A year and a half ago when Dr. Robert Glenn, a psychiatrist with the University of Texas Medical School,
came to Dallas, he and his wife moved into 3525. "I
didn't know any better," he now says. "My colleagues
took a very negative attitude toward our living there.
I'm sure they must have thought we were terrible snobs.
I must say that I was inclined to agree with them when

we, along with the other tenants, received a gift of match boxes from the management which were inscribed, 'Home of the Social Lions.'" Dr. and Mrs. Glenn have since moved.

To accommodate these new people in the Turtle Creek area and to handle the traffic from Highland and University Park and from the north, the city decided a few years ago that Turtle Creek had to be widened. The decision set off one of the liveliest furors in recent city history and even brought on some picketing. Dallas is so starved for beauty spots that whenever a visitor came to town, he was always driven down that winding, narrow street known as Turtle Creek. At certain times of the year, such as azalea time, it was especially beautiful and even gave the visitor the erroneous impression that Dallas is a green and flowering city.

In any case, the protests made about the widening of Turtle Creek stirred up headlines but did not in the least affect the wheels of progress. The street has indeed been widened, the high-rise apartments have been built, the Spa is in bustling operation, IBM is on one corner, and this residential area looks as though it has seen its best day. Some of the high-rise buildings, such as 3525 and the new Terrace Apartments over on Maple Avenue, not far away, are quite handsome. Others, such as the buildings which are replacing the old Jesuit high school, manage to give the impression that the inhabitants all live in cells. In any case, Dallas' most charming street is changing fast, and not to everyone's taste.

The second large group of luxury apartments inhabited by people of influence in the community is located on Preston Road and Northwest Highway, or just about in the middle of the north-south perimeter of The Establishment area. The area is surrounded by a wall, and residents refer to themselves as living "behind the wall." None of the buildings has any particular distinction but the apartments are roomy and comfortable and average out probably to around $300 to $350 a month, with some running as high as $800.

In this area, couples with children are not welcome and if you do see a little boy around one of the swimming pools, he is almost surely a resident's grandchild. Younger couples, with children and medium to lower incomes, live in apartment projects such as the one off Inwood built by the I & L Development Company. Usually these are older apartments and the rents are down around $110 or $120 a month. They are small, and the older ones have air conditioning units rather than central air conditioning. The newer ones are of course air conditioned—as is nearly everything in Dallas, including automobiles and even a few garages.

But to the sociologist, the psychologist and any other student of American mores in the mid-twentieth century, the most interesting apartments in the city are those that rent in a range from $150 to $250 a month. The overwhelming majority of them are occupied by single people in their twenties and thirties, living two, three and even four to an apartment. Buildings of such apartments have sprung up like some new plant throughout the entire city, but especially to the north and the east. Gaston Avenue, which once was the site of the city's finest old homes, now looks at night like a junior-sized Miami Beach.

The names of the buildings are all exotic. There are the Nassau, the Calypso, the Mediterranean, the Antilles, the Dauphine, the Continental, the Riviera and so on. They are all dramatically lighted and seem to promise strange and exotic pleasures. One such apartment house, the Columbian, got a radio commercial started on which a suggestive female voice promised, "Living is fun at the Columbian."

A great number of airline stewardesses are stationed in Dallas. They are all single, by definition. Nearly all of them live in apartments such as those just described, and as a result the phrase "stewardess apartments" is current. It is hardly a fair one; it simply means that there is a high prevalence of single young women who are secretaries, stenographers, models, salesgirls and receptionists living in the buildings.

Life in these apartments centers during the warm weather around the ever-present swimming pool. There

music is piped in, people meet each other, romances begin and end, parties begin and end and the sociologist
takes notes. Some of the apartments even have their own
private clubs for residents only.

Once I talked with a landlady who, as most of the
managers do, lived in one of the apartments in her project. She was the only person over thirty-five in the
building (she was in her sixties) and she had a high
interest in the affairs of her tenants. "It's like geometry,"
she told me. "I have four girls living in apartment 2507.
One of them is going with 3431, another with 2787, another with 3431 down the street and the last one, I think,
goes with my whole first floor. The boys upstairs in 4360,
they go with each other. So, you draw all the lines of
the radius and then some day something happens and
you start erasing them and drawing them all over again.
Fascinating, no?"

The apartment dwellers in such buildings have become known as the "suitcase set." They comprise the
most mobile of the various populations of Dallas. Literally, many of them will move into an apartment for
two months and move out of it to a newer one for another three or four months, moving again to a third location shortly afterward. These people can live out of a
suitcase and since many of the new apartments offer
a month's free rent, they can save money. This mobility
is, of course, the bane of the telephone company's

existence and on an apartment avenue like Gaston, telephone people are among the busier citizens.

The people who live in these $150 to $250-a-month
apartments comprise a sizable percentage of the population of Dallas. Yet they take almost no part at all in
the city's affairs. A high percentage of them never vote,
even in Presidential years. Their names are not on the
roster of any of the city's thousands of committees. They
do not go to concerts, they do not go to museums, they
do not go to the theater and about one in ten could tell
you the name of the county judge (Lew Sterrett). They
pay income tax and the sales tax and, if they own a car,
they pay property tax on it. Most of the men do own
cars, most of the girls do not. They are a faceless crowd
but there are enough of them to make up the third city.

The fourth city of Dallas has the fewest inhabitants:
this is downtown Dallas. Almost no one lives there. By
day it is a hustling salesman city of several hundred
thousand. They stream in from the north, the west, the
east and the south, between eight and nine in the morning, and they stream out again between five and six in
the evening. Walking through the streets of downtown
Dallas in the midst of a business day, one has the impression of health, activity and the sense of purpose.
Because of natural gas, it is an exceedingly clean city
and the campaigns against litterbugs work well.

The sense of growth is impressive. Since the war, Dallas has added more downtown office space than any city in America outside of New York. Everywhere you look, there is building and the sense of optimism projected by it is contagious. As in all other material ways, the city has shown strength and vision in its building programs. Out in the suburbs, huge new developments like Raymond Nasher's North Park are going up at a cost of hundreds of millions of dollars.

Suburban development has been explosive, as it has throughout most of America. But whereas some other cities have allowed the downtown area to stagnate and become a major problem, Dallas has protected its investment in downtown by a balanced program. Construction parallels itself in the suburbs and downtown. The Murchison brothers—Clint Jr. and John—have announced a tremendous plan for the western part of the downtown area which is at present a bit on the sleazy side and getting sleazier. To enable the Murchisons to build streets on several levels, the City Council has altered its air rights and its underground rights.

In spite of the building program, there are the usual ramshackle areas you find in most American cities. Across from the famous Neiman-Marcus store on Commerce Street is a fifth-rate short-order and beer place and a collection of other run-down and disreputable looking business establishments. A Gospel Mission gathers up its human outcasts nightly half a block from the store. The big downtown motion picture theaters are on Elm Street which progresses east into a long line of pawnshops. The only major park in the city in the downtown area is on deep south Ervay, a glum, run-down area, visited as seldom as possible by the responsible citizenry. At night the park attracts drunks and perverts and is not the kind of park where a nice young man takes his nice young lady to court.

By six o'clock in the evening the downtown area changes its character completely. The clubs and restaurants which were bustling at noon are almost empty. The people on the streets have come from the Sheraton, the Statler-Hilton, the Baker and the Adolphus. They are conventioneers for Dallas is a big convention city and they have been cooped up in meetings all day and now they are out walking the streets to find some fun.

They have dinner in the Empire Room at the Statler-Hilton or in the Century Room of the Adolphus and watch a floor show or they can journey up to Abe's Colony Club on Commerce Street whose star attraction is a stripper act called "Chris Colt and her 45's." They can go to Barney Weinstein's Theater Lounge and watch Nikki Joye in action; if it's a Friday, the Theater Lounge will have its amateur night in addition to the regular show. Amateur night has become a hot attraction in the strip joints and is found hilarious by most audiences.

To many, it is a strange and sickly thing of sadness, but it is popular. Of course the visitor could until recently go to Jack Ruby's Carousel Club.

Many visitors to the city desert it (as do the residents) in the evening and go to the suburbs for dinner carrying their bottles in a brown paper sack. They go to the Old Warsaw, Arthur's, The Beefeater, Mario's or one of half a dozen other restaurants scattered throughout the suburban area. In Texas it is socially unacceptable to walk into a restaurant or club carrying a bare bottle. It is always wrapped in a brown paper sack and if a visitor has not thought to do this, the headwaiter will do it for him.

At midnight, when everything closes, the police prowl the streets looking for stray drunks and cart them up to "High Five," the drunk tank. Veteran alcoholics escape this by journeying down to the viaducts at the west end of the city and spend the warm nights there with a bottle of cheap wine.

By one in the morning, downtown Dallas is deserted except for a few all-night coffee shops, open to the night workers and the police.

Most of the people who built and manage downtown Dallas live in the fifth city: fashionable North Dallas. (Some live in two virtual islands near the center of the city—Highland and University Parks—which are both

entirely surrounded by the city but are separate incorporated townships.)

The building rate in North Dallas has been phenom-
enal over the past twenty years. Whole sections that
were farmland and simple prairie have turned into housing developments involving homes which cost from $35,-
000 to $100,000. Ten years ago a prominent builder said
to me, "I sometimes wonder how far north these nuts
will go in order to be chic. I have a feeling it's St. Louis."

South Dallas remains, as it has for years, slum and
semi-slum area. East Dallas grows modestly, and Oak
Cliff, helped by the influx of blue-collar workers in industry to the west, has consistent population increases.
Fashionable Dallas has exploded to the north, but even
to the north there is geographic stratification.

To over-simplify, one might say that a family with an
income of $25,000 a year or better will endeavor to live
somewhere between the beginning of Turtle Creek
Boulevard and Forest Lane, a distance of about eleven
miles, and between Central Expressway to the east and
Midway Road to the west, a distance of about four
miles. With a few exceptions, most of the men and
women who control the destiny of Dallas live in the
over-$25,000-a-year section. This is the headquarters of
The Establishment. To the east and west, the houses
are smaller and they vary in price from, say, $13,000 up
to $35,000. In The Establishment area, the lower-priced

housing is probably based around $20,000, but the high-priced housing can run, for a single home, into hundreds of thousands of dollars and there are a number of homes on which more than a million dollars has been spent.

For a builder to erect a speculative house to sell for $100,000 is not in the least unusual. While he may not sell it in a weekend, he is usually not stuck with it. Builders like Ben Rosenthal and Hal Anderson think nothing of putting up large scale developments consisting of homes, each of which must sell for $60,000 or $70,000 and up.

In the suburban areas, life is probably similar to suburban life throughout the United States, and the difference between Establishment and non-Establishment areas is a matter of degree. For instance, Dallas is an automobile city. People do not commute to and from work by train—they drive. The wealthier families have two, three or four cars (one man has eight, since he dislikes the financial beating he takes on trade-ins) and the less wealthy own a single car: the husband gets into a car pool or sometimes his wife drives him down and picks him up.

The wealthy families have servants daily, though servants in Dallas as elsewhere are harder and harder to find; the less wealthy have a maid twice a week or so. Almost without exception, the servants are Negroes and, in recent years, there have been fewer and fewer

Negroes willing to take domestic work. As a result, one finds servants like Robbie, a big, strong, soft-voiced Negro who works parties only. He will be at the William Hudsons' on Friday night, the Jake L. Hamons' on Saturday night, the Dallas Cowboys Club on Sundays before the football game, and perhaps the Clint Murchisons' for supper after the game. (The evening meal is usually "supper" in Oak Cliff, "dinner" in North Dallas, unless it is after the theater or on Sundays.) Socially, Robbie goes more places than anyone.

The men get up early, go to work early, lunch early and return home late in Dallas. Despite popular legend, it is not a town of ease, luxury and a slow pace. It is a working town and its Establishment men, between attention to their businesses and civic work, will go step for step with any of the New Yorkers with whom I grew up. Still, Dallas gives the impression of a slower pace because its people seem friendly and, on the surface, hospitable. Men always stop for a word or two on the streets, and people seem genuinely glad to see other people. It is a first-name city, more than are the older, eastern cities. If I am twenty-five years old, and some friends have a little boy of six, he will call me Warren; when he is fifteen and I am thirty-four, he will call me Mr. Leslie; but when he is thirty and I am forty-nine, he will again call me Warren. By this time, we will be working on the same committees, going to the same parties and doing other things in common. It is a pleasant way to live, and it keeps the older men young.

In spite of the fact that they work hard, Dallas people love to give parties, and social life between the end of October and the first of May can be exhausting. This is the season of the various charity balls and of the debutante parties. When parents can be persuaded to allow their daughters to come out, they insure the young girls and themselves of about four months of sheer hell—acquired at ruinous expense. Debutantes in Dallas are introduced to society by the Idlewild Club, a men's organization. There is a huge ball toward the end of October, and from that moment until activity trails off in February there are luncheons, brunches, teas, dinner dances, cocktail parties and other balls, until the senses reel.

This same pounding hospitality is sometimes offered to visiting celebrities, such as a famous conductor who may be in town for a couple of weeks, or an opera star or a writer. Once, after a week of luncheons, cocktail parties and dinners, the English writer, J. B. Priestley, spied a literary colleague over in a corner. He walked over, offered his hand and said, "Dr. Livingstone, I presume."

Entertaining for visitors is usually a part of women's boards' duties. The Dallas Symphony Orchestra, for example, gives a party for every guest artist on its sub-scription series. The entertainment committee simply assigns somebody to give the party. Unless the couple is to be out of town or something catastrophic has hap-pened, they are expected to comply and they do, gra-ciously and handsomely. At this kind of fairly large party there is safety in numbers. It is easy to give a party for fifty for T. S. Eliot, but much harder to find eight people who might interest him over an evening. If and when such a party were organized, however, it would interest foreign observers, who think Texans eat meat with their hands, to know that the food would usually be excellent and the wines well chosen and properly served. There are some first-class cooks in private homes in Dallas and plenty of hostesses who can themselves fix up an excellent coq au vin or cassoulet.

Wines have skyrocketed in sales over the past fifteen years. When I first came to Dallas, good wines seldom accompanied dinner; today it is unusual when one is not offered wine. Texans, who are even poorer linguists than other Americans, may murder the pronunciation of a Chambertin Clos de Bèze, but they know what it is and they drink it and serve it to their friends. One is actually more likely to get a great wine in Texas than in New York. New Yorkers, who have been drinking wine longer, often pay less for a good wine. Texans, not sure that they know it all, consult a good merchant and pay more for what is safely the best. This philosophy has enabled a wine distributor like Tony LaBarba to build himself a home which fits right in with the best in The Establishment area.

In New York, society used to be divided into two groups, old guard and café society. In Dallas, the old guard would represent money and position achieved in pre-boom days, mostly from cotton and ranching and the older financial institutions. Café society (which is a misnomer since there are no cafés to speak of) would be the newer money and influence. Money itself cannot buy a man into this group, which comprises much of The Establishment. Operational money usually can. A wildcatter who becomes suddenly rich and builds himself a big home will be discussed by the group (especially in terms of how much he spent on his home) but will not be a member of it until he has demonstrated that he means to use his money and its power for the good of the city. A man like James V. Ling, who came out of nowhere to build the huge Ling-Temco-Vought electronics complex, will be accepted quickly. It will be assumed that he has a stake in Dallas and that it has a stake in him.

Another even quicker device for joining the world of the Dallas Establishment, is to have a good name somewhere else. When Dedo Du Pont, of the famous Wilmington family, married Baron Kidd of Dallas, she was proposed for various civic groups before she had even arrived in Dallas.

But to many people who arrive in Dallas without the above qualifications, the city seems cold.

"At first, you think it's wonderful," a young doctor's wife from the East said to me. "The people are friendly and cheerful. They don't even lock their cars and neither do I any more! And they say, 'We've got to get together.' But then, 'we' never do. The phone never rings. They just don't mean it."

I asked one of the city's prominent women about this. "We do mean it, a little," she said, thoughtfully. "But there's so little time. I'm sure the people she met have her in the back of their mind. But, in the back. In the front are all the things that have to be done, and the fact that Sam is so tired at night. New people are an effort. It's easier with old friends."

To the north, then, lies Establishment Dallas, surrounded on all sides by people who wish to be in it, by people who do not wish to be in it, by people who vaguely resent it, and by a good many people who couldn't care less but are glad it is there because its money takes care of their city.

It should be noted that a large percentage of the

business leadership does not even live in Dallas. Instead, they live either in Highland Park or University Park, two incorporated townships just north of the center of town which are entirely surrounded by Dallas. In other words, the 11,000 residents of Highland Park and the 23,000 residents of University Park have their own school systems, police departments, town halls and mayors. The residents earn their livings from Dallas, but they do not pay Dallas taxes and, living in their little islands, they are immune to some of the problems that face Dallas. There is no school integration in the Park Cities—as these two enclaves are often called—because no Negroes live there. Either community would buy a house at triple its value to prevent a Negro's moving into it; Negro servants, of course, arrive daily to take care of the white houses. There are no slums, and social welfare doesn't exist because there is no need for it. The residents enjoy all of the assets and share none of the disadvantages of living in a growing city.

Some of the Highland and University Park citizens find their situation indefensible, and a few—like Eugene McElvaney, one of the best known bankers in the city—have had the courage to speak out publicly against it. But few of their fellow residents have shown any inclination to allow annexation by Dallas proper.

To many critics, the Park Cities community typifies some of Dallas' worst faults—an atmosphere of smugness, a lack of social conscience and a lack of involvement with problems of the total community, all of which leads to a brand of self-satisfied ultra-conservatism that has been the trademark of Dallas. Yet many of the city's leaders are pleased to live on their island.

The people of Dallas live well ($6,188 is the median income). Their standards are as good or better than those of most Americans, and they can expect the standards to improve because of continuing growth. Most of them are pleased to be where they are. An extraordinary number of them love their city and would be loath to leave it. In short, they are a prosperous community. And if they have faith in their leaders, it is because these men have brought them this prosperity.

3 | The "yes or no" men

The most influential leader of Dallas was the late R. L. (Bob) Thornton, chairman of the Mercantile National Bank and one of the most remarkable men Dallas ever produced. He died recently at the age of eighty-three, but in his heyday of leadership he had a magnetism and color that has not been replaced. During the thirties

and forties and most of the fifties he was the most powerful man in town though he neither had nor wanted the
influence of an Amon Carter in Fort Worth, which was
practically a one-man city. Among other things, Thornton served four terms as mayor of the city of Dallas,
but—far more important than that—he organized the
decision-makers in Dallas. In 1937 he brought about the
founding of the Citizens' Council.

Thornton was an exceptional man, even by Dallas
standards. He was born in a dugout in Hico County and
he and his brother argued until his brother's death about
which one was the older. He had little schooling and he
used to mispronounce English with great enthusiasm. It
was Thornton who coined the phrase "the dydamic men
of Dallas," and he was always talking about things that
were "tremenjus," "stupenjus" or whatever. This was,
of course, all an act. He was a big, rangy fellow with
quick, shrewd eyes and a shock of white hair. He had
enormous charm and humor and a gift of phrase, and his
use of language was simply one of the assets in his projection of personality.

"If it's a do meetin', I'm goin'," he used to say. "If it's
a don't meetin', I'm stayin' home."

And he insisted, "Ain't nobody built anything big
enough in Dallas. As soon as it's built, it's outgrowed."

He loved activity and the swirl of events around him.
Once he said, "All these people complainin' about traffic

downtown. Hell, it's easy—you got big business, you got traffic. You got traffic, you got a problem. If you don't want a problem, you go to Forney, Texas. In Forney, Texas, they got no problem, no traffic and no business."

He was for years the president of the State Fair of Texas, which is the nation's biggest state fair and attracts more than 2,500,000 visitors annually. Outside of Dallas itself, the fair was the single dearest thing to his heart. "The State Fair of Texas has greener grass, bluer lagoons, and higher skyrockets than any other fair in the world," he once said. "It's got a cash register under every bush, and we're plantin' more bushes."

During his years of power, whatever he did for Dallas was measurable in dollars and cents. Once he even headed a fund-raising drive for the Dallas Symphony Orchestra, an organization of whose virtues or demerits he was totally unaware, as he had never attended a concert. As soon as he had exacted a promise from the management that he would never be *asked* to attend a concert, he went out to raise the money. "Coldest snake I ever touched," he remarked during the middle of his campaign. Nevertheless, he did raise the money. He was convinced that a symphony orchestra was absolutely necessary to the economic growth of Dallas and he sold the orchestra on that basis and on that basis alone. In doing so, he gave a pattern to the raising of money for various artistic endeavors in Dallas.

Most of the leaders of arts campaigns begin by stating that they themselves couldn't care less about the arts, but that it is good for the city to have them. In my seventeen years in Dallas, I have never heard a man try to raise money for the orchestra on the basis that he loves music. Music lovers and money raisers anywhere are normally not the same breed of cat. To raise money in Dallas and in most American cities, you have to have money; you must have trading ability. "Now listen, Dick," an opera man will say, "you are going to be calling me about this hospital drive you're on and I'm going to help you exactly in proportion to how you help me with the opera."

Moral and artistic values do not often enter into these matters, even when the matters themselves are issues of morality or art.

This is important to understand in any examination of the influential group known as the Dallas Citizens' Council. Scores of articles have been written about the Council since the assassination and one can get the impression that its members rule Dallas spiritually as well as financially. This is nonsense. The Citizens' Council is a collection of dollars represented by men. The men themselves shift in importance, but one thing characterizes all of them: they are all able to commit their companies to civic expenditures. They do not have to consult with boards or advisers. Being the heads of businesses, they

have the authority to take action. Thornton, who originated the Council, had wanted to call it the "Yes or No
Council," but he was overruled.

In many American cities, power descends from a
small group of influential businessmen to the city council. What distinguishes the Dallas power group from
others is that it is organized, it has a name, it is not artic-
ulately opposed and it was highly publicized even before the events of November. In earlier days the publicity was favorable; now it is critical. Many articles have
pointed out that Dallas is run by a group which has no
mandate from the people and which is not subject to recall.

Not even the most sensitive member of the Council
will deny that it has strong influence on the affairs of the
city. But the term "oligarchy" carries an implication of
government for selfish interest. This irritates men like
Erik Jonsson, chairman of Texas Instruments, past president of the Citizens' Council and now mayor of Dallas.

"You know damned well it's a benevolent organization," he said recently. "Time and again I've seen men
do things that were contrary to their best interests for
the good of the city. This is a competitive city and these
fellows will fight like hell all day long against each other,
but then they'll sit down at dinner and try to figure out
a way to bring a new business here, or build an auditorium, or whatever. Look at Thornton and Florence, a

couple of bankers. [The late Fred Florence, chief of the Republic National Bank.] They scratched hard trying to land a new account or get a big loan, but they worked together like a couple of brothers on Dallas business."

Jonsson also was disturbed over an article which stated that nothing in Dallas ever got done without the approval of the Citizens' Council. "That sounds as though we wave a wand, and all of a sudden it's done. That's nonsense. If a school bond issue is needed, they come to see us and tell us what it's about. If we think they're right, we say that we'll help them try to sell it to the people. That's all we can do."

It is indeed all the Council can do, but it is an important job and the Council can do it well. Any proposition in any city runs up against a certain amount of voting strength which automatically opposes it—automatically, because these voters always oppose everything. "And they always vote," Jonsson says. "The 'ayes' will stay home unless you sell them on taking the trouble to vote."

On some matters, the Council can act independently of voters. If the symphony orchestra runs out of money, as is common, it can come before the Council to be bailed out, and so far it always has been bailed out. The Citizens' Council can usually be persuaded to allocate funds to some urgently needed project, as a rule without much vocal opposition, since the projects involved are usually sound.

The Council is nominally nonpolitical, but its sister organization, the Citizens' Charter Association, is purely political. Its simple purpose is to find the best men possible for the City Council, then to persuade them to run and finally to elect them. When it succeeds in getting them elected, as it usually does, the councilmen are beholden to the Charter Association, which is closely related to the Citizens' Council. This is the system by which the nonpolitical Citizens' Council exercises a crushing political influence in Dallas.

It doesn't always work. Years ago J. B. (Tiste) Adoue decided to be mayor of Dallas, as his father had been before him. In those days, mayors were not elected, they were appointed by the elected City Council. Adoue, the best vote-getting name on the ticket, led all the Charter candidates home and confidently expected to be appointed mayor. Unfortunately, though respected as a banker, he was considered something of a maverick by his associates on the Citizens' Council. "You never could be sure what Tiste would do," one of them told me. "He had his own ideas about everything, didn't always go along with the group." For that reason the City Council astounded the whole city, especially Adoue, by appointing Wallace Savage, a man who could be expected to cooperate fully with the Citizens' Council. Snorting like a bull, the white-haired Adoue went through the roof.

"Double-cross!" he yelled and vowed to take his fight to the people. He did, and the voters emphatically backed him.

Since then mayors of Dallas have been elected by the people—a serious blow, one would think, to The Establishment. Actually, it hasn't turned out that way. The most recent mayor, Earle Cabell, beat the Charter Association once and came pretty close to beating it twice. His political philosophy and that of the Charter Association are virtually indistinguishable, and he would certainly have been a Charter candidate the first time, except that he made the mistake of running before they wanted him to. Bob Thornton, going into his fourth term, beat Cabell. When Thornton retired, Cabell ran against another Charter candidate but one who did not inspire much enthusiasm from his backers. Cabell won, probably with as many Charter as non-Charter votes.

When Earle Cabell recently retired as mayor in order to run for Congress, it was announced that J. Erik Jonsson had accepted the job. There had been no prior announcement that Jonsson had been offered the job. Five councilmen simply went out to ask him. They came back and announced that he had accepted.

At lunch the next day Larry Kelly, executive director of the Dallas Civic Opera, laughed about it. "I think we have the only city in the world where it could happen," he said. "Any other place there'd be a thousand pickets down there protesting it. *Somebody*, for *some* reason, has to be against him. But—not a peep in Dallas."

Actually, there was a peep. The councilmen who weren't invited to join the delegation of five announced that they were indignant; more at not being invited, one suspects, than at the choice.

Legally this transfer of power was possible because Jonsson will fill an unexpired term. Practically, it makes sense. Jonsson, if he had had to run, could probably have beaten anyone who might have run against him. He seems a fine choice.

But even the good Lord had people against him. Not Erik Jonsson in Dallas.

The roots of the powerful Citizens' Council in Dallas go back to 1936, when the city became the site of the Texas Centennial. Dallas' chief weapon in the battle for the Centennial had been the lure of $3,500,000 it offered in support of the fair, but raising it had been slow work. One problem was that it took so long to get an answer from companies that had been asked to give the money.

"There was no organization," Bob Thornton said. "We had to have men who could underwrite. . . . Sometimes you'd get a bunch together. They couldn't say yes or no. We didn't have time for no proxy people—what we needed was men who could give you the box score. Then I saw the idea. Why not organize the 'yes' and 'no' people? So I went by to see Nate Adams."

Adams at that time was head of the First National Bank, then the biggest and now the second biggest bank in Dallas. Adams agreed that it made sense, and the Citizens' Council was founded.

It was then an organization of one hundred men representing companies which could provide cash. (Now its membership is about two hundred.) Proxy people were not allowed to attend their meetings. In Thornton's words, "If you don't come, you ain't there." The members paid light dues and the twenty-four directors put in enough extra money so that they could eat lunch together once a month. (As a matter of fact, the dues are so light that the Council is now broke corporately, though scarcely individually.) Membership in the Council was restricted to chief executive officers of major corporations. There were and still are no doctors, lawyers, clergymen, psychologists, sociologists, writers, painters, newspaper reporters or educators—except for Dr. Willis Tate, the head of Southern Methodist University, who was apparently considered chief executive officer of a business organization.

As a dollar group, the Council acts on the simple basis of what is and what is not good for business growth in the community. When it approves something, it can act quickly and positively.

Years ago, Holland McCombs told the story of the move of Chance Vought Aircraft (now the enormous electronics complex known as Ling-Temco-Vought) to Dallas from Connecticut. Rex Beisel, then the head of Chance Vought, suddenly realized that the runways at Dallas' airport were not long enough for the company's purposes. He called D. A. Hulcy, then the head of the Citizens' Council, and told him that the runways would have to be two thousand feet longer or Chance Vought would be unable to move. Three hours and forty minutes later, Hulcy telephoned Beisel that the City Council had been persuaded to call an emergency meeting and the $256,000 had been voted for the runways. Work would begin Monday morning. Out of this phone call came an enterprise which now employs more than 20,000 people in Dallas.

When the city badly needed a new downtown hotel, the Citizens' Council approved debentures worth $1,-500,000 to encourage the Statler Hotels to build one. Statler, then headed by Arthur Douglas, did build one and the site was chosen late one night after a council dinner by Douglas, Bob Thornton and Stanley Marcus as they drove around the city together. Today it is one of the major landmarks of Dallas and (having been taken

over by Conrad Hilton) is one of the more profitable hotels in the Hilton chain.

The most serious problem confronting the Citizens'
Council in recent years has been the matter of integration.

Dallas, along with the other major Texas cities, should
not be equated with the deep South in terms of Negro-
white relationships. About 130,000 Negroes live in Dallas—a vastly lower percentage than in the troubled areas
of the deep South. Though there are incidents from time
to time in low-income areas where Negroes and whites
live close together, the racial situation has been controllable. Nevertheless, Dallas has a southern background
and a southern outlook toward integration.

Predictably, Dallas began by fighting the Supreme
Court decision through every legal means at its command. When these steps failed, as the city's leaders knew
they would, the Citizens' Council went into action. First
of all the city had gone through the legal steps not so
much out of a hope of winning, but for public relations
reasons. The citizenry had to be convinced that nothing
had been left undone in the effort to fight integration.
The second step was to present the Citizens' Council
with the proposal that integration, or at least token integration, should be accomplished efficiently and without incident.

A member of the Citizens' Council explained it to me this way: "Thornton just came up before us and told us what had happened in other cities. He told us how much business had suffered in Birmingham, New Orleans and the rest. He told us how much it would cost Dallas if we couldn't solve the problem quickly and peaceably. There was not a single piece of sentiment at the meeting. It was not an argument over whether Negroes should be integrated or not. It was simply a matter of dollars and cents. We ended up by giving him more money than they turned out to need."

It was a massive program under the direction of two members of the Council: C. A. Tatum, president of the Dallas Power and Light Company, and Sam Bloom, president of the advertising agency bearing his name. They worked long, hard hours with the Negro leadership and the white people of Dallas who would have to accept a new era. Schools were not the only problem. Hotels, restaurants, stores and other public facilities also had to integrate. If they did not, the nonviolent sit-in demonstrations would certainly take place in Dallas as they had through the South. The whole program took about two years and of course it is still going on. Integration is by no means complete in Dallas and the Negroes continue to press for greater help in their uphill climb.

Under the direction of Tatum and other Citizens'

Council representatives, Sam Bloom handled the me-
chanics. He produced a film called "Dallas at the Cross-
roads" to show to church and club groups of every
kind the consequences of nonacceptance of integration.
He enlisted the support of the newspapers, radio stations, television stations, the clergy, the club officers,
labor unions, businessmen and the police. It was a mas-
terful job of infecting a total community with belief in
an idea repugnant to it.

"If you're going to sell a concept to a community,"
Bloom says, "you have to make it palatable. When we
showed people what had happened in other cities, our
concept became palatable."

The integration so far achieved in Dallas has taken
place without any unpleasantness. Even at Neiman-
Marcus, where a single outraged customer can cost the
store $50,000 or more a year, the integration of its fash-
ionable Zodiac Restaurant was accomplished smoothly.
On a day prearranged with the Negro leadership, four
Negroes, two men and two women, simply came in and
had lunch. Store executives thought they might get a reaction of several hundred letters, but they actually received fewer than thirty, some of them heartily approving the action. Only one charge account was closed, and
it was reopened within the week. The appearance of
Negroes shopping in the store and lunching in the restaurant scarcely raises an eyebrow today. On the sur-

face, at least, integration in Dallas was a brilliant job of execution. It did not, of course, have a moral basis. An appeal to moral values could not have accomplished integration; only an appeal to material values.

The Council is so closely knit that one gets the impression that everything in town has the same board of directors; that the men leading the United Fund are the same who run the Civic Opera, who run the symphony, who run the new hospital drive and who run the state fair. While the observer would be wrong in that the boards are not identical, they certainly have overlapping memberships. This is embarrassing at times, especially when the opera and the symphony squabble about something and, looking around a board meeting of either, one realizes that half the board of the other is present.

This situation arises because these men have become key symbols in the community. In the old days, not only did the presence of Thornton and Fred Florence give stature to an organization, but if they were not present the organization *lost* status and its chances for success were dimmed. Today, J. Erik Jonsson is on the board of nearly everything not only because he contributes intelligence and often money (he and his Texas Instruments associates Eugene McDermott and Cecil Green have been among the city's great benefactors) but because his name gives every board solidity and authority. Taking it a step further, his election as mayor gives the city of Dallas solidity and authority.

Today, in addition to Jonsson, there are a few other men whose support in any civic project is an absolute necessity. Among them would be Robert Cullum, head of a food store chain and of the chamber of commerce; C. A. Tatum, president of the power company and chief leader of the successful integration action; James Aston, head of the Republic National Bank; Robert Stewart, president of the First National Bank; and Les Potter, head of the gas company. The bankers are present not only because of the personal influence of the men but because in any civic project the bank "clearing house," an organization of all Dallas banks, must approve; if it doesn't, the utilities will not go along either. Without the banks and the utilities the project is dead, unless—as almost never happens—somebody wants to finance it himself.

These leading men are all about fifty, with the exception of Stewart, who is in his thirties and is generally considered the light of the future in Dallas. Nearly all of them are enlightened conservatives. Standing with them, but to one side, is Stanley Marcus, the president of Neiman-Marcus and a liberal—rather a lonely thing to be in Dallas. Somewhere between Marcus and most of the others stands Charles Meyer, head of Sears Roebuck in the area. Finally, a little in the background these days, stands the elderly Karl Hoblitzelle, a tall, gray, soft-spoken man who built the great Interstate Theater chain and is board chairman of the Republic Bank. Though Hoblitzelle does not take as active a part as he once did, his positive influence is extremely helpful and his negative influence, should he care to use it, would probably doom anything of which he disapproved.

If these nine men agree on something, and if at the same time the newspapers, led by Joe Dealey (the *News*) and James Chambers (the *Times-Herald*) also agree, this automatically means that the two Dallas television stations will agree, since they are both owned by the newspapers. In the end, it means that the rest of the Citizens' Council will agree and so, eventually, will the rest of the city.

Taking this a step further, I would guess that if everybody were out of town except Tatum, Cullum and Jonsson, joined by either one of the bankers, the same process could take place, only a little more slowly.

Dallas, then, is not run by a power elite of two hundred; it is run—or strongly led—by a group of at most ten, at fewest three, men. One could say that they carry a heavy load: a city of three-quarters of a million people, with a metropolitan area of a million and a quarter.

It should be understood that none of this takes place

without argument and dissension. Neither the ten nor the three men could get anything done which the others considered a mistake. No member of the Citizens' Council is *told* what to do by any other member. Instead, a proposition is submitted by the leaders, and the others comment. If the proposition seems sound, it is approved. If it does not seem sound, it is not disapproved; it is simply not approved. No action is taken, and the proposition is dead.

What has made this system work for Dallas is that the proposition is normally sound, and that individual selfish interest is simply not tolerated in this group. The common selfish interest is in the growth and economic betterment of Dallas, which redounds to the individual welfare. But, in those cases where individual welfare has seemed to dictate the proposition—or opposition to the proposition—the other men see it immediately.

"We know each other pretty well and we know the city pretty well," one of the saltier members said to me. "If there's a private buck involved, most of us can smell it at twenty feet."

These men of Dallas are exceptional by any standards I know in America. They understand power structures, they are intelligent, they are devoted to their city, they check and balance each other adroitly and they are superb salesmen. They have made Dallas an economic boom town. It is no wonder that they are shocked and resentful when their city is suddenly attacked and vilified by the press and the world.

In 1963, the Citizens' Council was forced to recognize the fact that the arts in Dallas were in trouble. It was decided to form a community arts fund, the benefits of which would be distributed among the orchestra, the Civic Opera, the Metropolitan Opera (which makes an annual visit to Dallas at a deficit), the summer musicals and the Dallas Theater Center. Unfortunately, investigation showed that these organizations, proudly led by the symphony and the Civic Opera, were already more than $700,000 in debt—in *past* debt. Anyone who has ever tried to raise money for anything knows that it is one thing to raise money for the future and another, far tougher thing to raise money for the past.

Twenty-five Dallas men met each morning at the Petroleum Club at nine o'clock. They went about raising the money from private interests the way Americans traditionally have: "Here's Paul's card; who can get it out of Paul? Who's got an in with Sam? Jimmy ought to give more than that; let's get back to him."

In an astonishing performance, these twenty-five men raised more than $700,000 to pay off *past* debts of the arts in Dallas. They raised the money from 129 firms or individuals, a pitifully small number in comparison to the total population, and even in comparison to the wealthy population.

With past debts paid up, the Community Arts Fund went to the people to support their orchestra, opera, theater center, summer musicals and the Metropolitan's annual visit. The budget was about $650,000, and this time the effort failed. Only about $360,000 could be raised for the future, as opposed to the $700,000 for the past debts. Here, too, the figures are interesting. Four hundred individuals or firms gave $700 or more, and 611 gave an average of $20. In the two drives, then, less than 1,200 people—considerably less, since there were many duplications—gave over a million dollars. The figures are impressive in two ways: the amount given per capita was abnormally high, the total number of givers was abnormally low—less than a quarter of 1 per cent of the population, less than half the audience at an average concert.

Most of the criticism now being directed at this form of city government has been on the basis that Dallas is being run by the selfish few for the selfish few. This is simply unfactual; it is a superficial observation made by the reporters who travel through town with the wind and leave with a little knowledge—which, as we all know, is a dangerous thing.

The major thing to be said about the Citizens' Council's failures is that it has done its material city-building so well that it has been expected to do everything else just as well, including a lot of things it is totally un-equipped to do. One kind of man, for instance, is experienced and expert in the techniques of bringing a new industry to town. It does not follow that he also understands the necessity for four additional first violins for the orchestra. This kind of man is proud of the enormous population gains his city has made and vaguely aware that they have caused problems. But when he is told that one pregnant Negro woman out of three never sees a doctor and that a second sees one only once during her pregnancy, he is perhaps dismayed but he is out of his field. And when somebody tells him that in Dallas only one unmarried mother out of twenty-nine gets any kind of help for herself and the child (except obstetrical), his first reaction may be that she ought to get married.

Sam Bloom, the big, graying advertising man who executes many Citizens' Council policies, is one of those who think the Council has done well the things it could see and understand. The city's trouble areas, he thinks, exist because the city has been asking wisdom and enlightenment and a kind of moral vision not to be found, as a rule, in a businessmen's organization oriented toward the practical use of cash.

Sitting at the Dallas Club recently, surrounded by many of the people he was talking about, Bloom reflected: "After all, they've created a clean city, if not necessarily an enlightened one. Whenever they've understood the need of something, they've done it. But of course in lots of ways they've lacked the ability to see what was wrong. When you get to discussing real problems like West Dallas slums, you usually do a lot more stirring up than you do changing. Normally, people want to discuss their problems but they don't want to live with them. They talk about them during the day and then at night they escape out to Highland Park or University Park, or the suburbs in general. I also get irritated at the intellectuals who try to put the whole thing in a test tube. You can't just analyze and discuss and all that sort of thing. You've got to stay with these things until something happens. That's why the intellectuals themselves have contributed something to the unrest because they're inclined to voice their displeasure, but they don't do much about it.

"One reason I think we've done so many good things and have so many blind spots is that the city was so completely man-made. And since it was man-made, there is a need for acceptance and approval among men here that is unique. It is necessary to be popular. For instance, it's no problem to get outstanding people to work on a committee for the Methodist Hospital, but for more controversial causes the leaders may lose popularity and approval. So, we have a lot of people around here who are cautious in exploring the areas which are not necessarily popular, like slum clearance, public housing, the United Nations and all the things you know about.

"Of course all of this is an American story as well as a Dallas story, and maybe now we are only beginning to get a maturing of democracy. Charity, after all, began in the church, and then it got too complicated for the church to handle and society had to take it on. But society hasn't yet faced its full responsibility for all these problems. It is one of the great challenges of a free people. Can we do it? We haven't always done it here. Maybe it's the first time a *people* has been faced with this kind of social challenge. Governments have done it and they may yet do it here. Despots have done it, but in America just plain people are being asked to do it, and when they don't we see the government moving in and doing it for us."

Bloom thinks that in attempts to keep up with the changing currents in Dallas, the Citizens' Council itself will one day change. "In holding to the money structure, the Council forfeited ideas and help in recognizing things it should have been doing and wasn't," he says.

He feels that non-cash people, like educators, professors, sociologists, psychologists, lawyers and doctors, will someday become a part of the governing body. If he is right, this will make for dramatic changes. The business community is tightly knit within itself, but its ties with the intellectual community are faint. To charges that the Citizens' Council is too inbred, Bloom, the realist, replies: "The progressive man, the man who is getting ahead, lives in the same kind of community as the other men who are getting ahead."

Human beings, Bloom feels, recognize and trust each other most readily when the symbols of their lives are similar—that is, when they live in the same kind of houses and neighborhoods, drive the same kind of cars, wear the same kind of clothes and send their children to the same kind of schools. The leadership of Dallas, like other people, seeks out its own kind. Bloom describes it, in part, this way:

"You look at this community and sometimes you think you can almost trace it back to the Highland Park Methodist Church. Tatum, Bob Cullum, Jim Chambers, and Felix McKnight over at the *Times-Herald*—lots of them go back to that one outfit. If you wanted to, you could go a step further and name the most powerful forces in Dallas. You'd have to say the Highland Park Methodist Church, the Highland Park Presbyterian Church, the Park Cities Baptist Church, the Republic National Bank, the First National Bank and, where there are Jews involved, they all belong to Temple Emanu-el.

"Believe me, you can't turn over a rock in this town when the members of these organizations don't crawl out. But hell, they all grew up together and they can predict each other. If it's inbred, it's not peculiar to Dallas. Out in Dayton, Ohio, the town leadership comes out of one of the country clubs. When the city was having a lot of trouble between the military at Wright Air Force Base and the civilians, they thought of going to Washington and a lot of other things. You know what they did? They just made the officers at the air base members of the country club. All of a sudden, symbols began to be understood and now everybody gets along so well that military men fight to get to Dayton."

The Citizens' Council, a nonpolitical, nonspiritual organization, finds itself continually involved in politics and in the moral (integration) and spiritual (the arts) life of the city. The Council is no more equipped to guide Dallas in these matters than a similar group of businessmen in Peoria or Kansas City or New York would be. Its influence has produced clean, graft-free city government, of which it is understandably proud. But it has not necessarily produced enlightened government, and somewhere along the way of its activities it seems to have lost the people. In most cities this would mean that the people would vote the Council members out; in Dallas they cannot be voted out because they have never been voted in.

What seems to me to have happened in Dallas is that the people have not been made angry, they have been made apathetic. They have the feeling that all will be well and that their leaders will take care of them. Only one fourth of the eligible voters bothered to vote on Cabell's housing plan. There are fewer than a thousand contributors to the Dallas Symphony Orchestra; in Houston, there are four thousand. Mental health and social welfare do not excite the citizenry because their leaders are not very excited. In the end, government by private club is government by *junta,* whether benevolent or not. Benevolent in Dallas, it has still lost for the city the values of debate, self-criticism and even the kind of new ideas which provides the balance Dallas so seriously needs.

4 | Absolutists: The third party

Any city which is as business-oriented as Dallas is likely
to be politically conservative. The fact that Dallas businessmen prefer the Republican Party to the Democratic
Party makes them exactly like other American businessmen. Dallas voted Democrat until 1952 only because
everyone in the South did. Even then it was a conservative, anti-union city. When Governor Allan Shivers

switched Texas to Eisenhower in 1952, Dallas went with him and has voted Republican in three Presidential elections and has elected its Republican congressman, Bruce Alger, for four terms. Still, there are many old ties to the Democrats that men don't give up easily. The result of this has been that in Dallas, as in Texas, the Democratic Party has been badly split between conservatives who wish to be Democrats and liberal loyal Democrats who voted for Kennedy out of conviction. When Senator John Tower, Republican, was elected over former Senator Bill Blakley, it was partly because loyal Democrats simply stayed home. Blakley was so close to Tower's conservativism that they hadn't anyone to vote for.

Lately, however, Dallas conservatism has begun to be looked upon as excessive even by other conservative business communities. The excesses have been given prominence by press coverage of incidents involving the far right. Actually, the people who go to Birch Society meetings, Major General Walker meetings and National Committee meetings comprise a small section of Dallas conservatives. They make a great deal of noise and they get themselves on front pages, but their numbers are not impressive. When the National Indignation Committee, for example, had its second meeting, in 1961, only about one hundred people showed up.

Another popular fallacy about Dallas is that it is run by oil millionaires who all belong to the extreme right wing. As we have seen by looking at the Citizens' Council, oil men don't run Dallas at all. They can have influence within the city if they show an interest in it. Paul Raigorodsky, an oil man, is chairman of the board of the Dallas Theater Center and had a great part in getting it built. Jake L. Hamon, an oil man, has served on the Citizens' Council for years and has the complete respect of his colleagues. The Murchison brothers, Clint Jr. and John, are just about to rebuild the western end of town with oil money. One of them owns the local National Football League team, the Dallas Cowboys, and their wives are on practically every civic committee in the city. There are others whose help is wanted and sought. But none of these men runs Dallas, and a great many oil men don't have any part at all in the city's activities. Oil men are traditionally rootless. If they happen to live in Dallas, it is not because the city is anything more than a home to them. In other words, they don't need it. Bankers, insurance men, retailers, utility people, all need the city in which they live; it feeds them. Oil men traditionally, with some exceptions, have not been a part of the Dallas Establishment.

The legends gain currency by the publicity given a man like H. L. Hunt, who is certainly one of the wealthiest men in America and whose name is certainly associated with Dallas. He was the founder of an ultra-conservative organization known as Facts Forum and the originator of an equally conservative radio program called "Life-Line." Mr. Hunt also wrote a novel called *Alpaca* about his theories on an ideal government, which would distribute votes according to the amount of taxes paid but would limit the income tax to a maximum of 25%. But in spite of his great wealth and his literary bent, the famous Mr. Hunt is not even a member of the Citizens' Council, and his advice about problems of the community is seldom sought.

Every city seems to have a built-in supply of fanatics, and Dallas probably has more than its share. But what it also has, which is of interest to the sociologist and the psychologist, is a seemingly inexhaustible supply of young and middle-aged people, many of them college-educated, who see black or white and literally nothing else. These are nice looking, pleasant, attractive people. Their children are handsome. They are open and friendly in business, they are hospitable, they attend church, and they keep a clean house. They live in Establishment and non-Establishment areas throughout the whole city. They are really a very attractive group until you discover that the human mind is for them an instrument for the projection rather than the reception of ideas.

Almost without exception, these are people who feel that their greatest enemy is not the Soviet Union or

Communist China, but the government of the United States. Their wives feel it even more fiercely. They feel that their worst enemies are other Americans who disagree with them. They are not equipped to deal with contradictory evidence; when it appears, they boo it and hiss it to make it go away. Their statements are positive and final; if one does not agree with them, one is in the enemy camp, at least temporarily. In other words, these people do not recognize any middle ground. To give in to the pressure of a new idea is weakness.

When you live in Texas for a while as a liberal, you know quickly what to talk about and what not to talk about in certain groups. During the Kennedy Administration, an expressed admiration for the President could literally ruin a dinner party. So could any objection to the policies and conduct of Republican congressman Bruce Alger.

In this kind of situation, with so many people believing so much the same thing and so strongly, radicalism is defined by distance, not direction. The radical moves with the mainstream, but he moves further.

Several years ago, my wife and I dined in the Old Warsaw restaurant in Dallas with the famous 'cellist, Gregor Piatigorsky, a huge, strapping man who still speaks with a Russian accent. Our talk concerned the Russian violinist David Oistrakh and other Russian artists who had made a success in the United States. Piatigorsky asked why none of them had played in Dallas, and I explained that the State Department had placed Dallas—and certain other American communities—off-limits to visiting Russian artists. The ban was in retaliation for a similar one in Russia as to where visiting Americans could perform. The 'cellist asked me whether the American ban might not be removed if Dallas requested it. I said I thought it might, but that I doubted that Dallas would ever request its removal.

"Why not?" he asked.

"Well, if Oistrakh played, I imagine there would be pickets and a big fight. It's also possible that the symphony would lose some of its financial support."

"But he's a violinist, not a politician," Piatigorsky said.

I told him some similar stories involving the Museum of Fine Arts and the controversy over hanging pictures by Picasso and Rivera. Piatigorsky shook his head: "What is it that people here fear so much?" he said.

When we were leaving, we stopped to say good night to the restaurant owner, Stanislaus Slawik, a mustached, distinguished looking former diplomat.

"I think," he said, smiling, "that you owe me money on your dinner tonight. Two tables of people walked out before their meal."

"Why?" I asked.

"They said they refused to sit in a restaurant and

listen to subversive talk," Slawik said. "One of them said he'd be damned if he'd have his soup sitting next to a bunch of Communists."

"You see what I mean?" I said to Piatigorsky, who is married to a Rothschild and is one of capitalist America's most successful concert artists; and who, at that moment, was looking as though he doubted his sanity.

The ban has since been removed, but Oistrakh has not yet played in Dallas.

At a recent meeting of a local chapter of the Parent-Teacher Association, a film was shown concerning some of the House Un-American Activities Committee activities in San Francisco. When it was over, there was loud applause, but a sociologist in the audience rose to his feet. He wished to point out, he said, that some of the events shown in the film were out of sequence; some of the things shown toward the end had actually preceded events shown at the beginning. He was booed and hissed back into his seat.

"I am constantly amazed," another man, Dr. Harry Martin, sociologist at the University of Texas Medical School, said, "at the number of people I meet in Dallas who cannot accept contradictory evidence. New facts which don't support old theories can't be facts, they seem to feel."

These are not, as a rule, the people who go around

striking or spitting at other people. But they are absolutists.

In his widely read New Year's Day advertisement, Stanley Marcus, president of Neiman-Marcus, wrote: "The [absolutist] is the man who thinks that he alone possesses wisdom, patriotism, and virtue, who recognizes no obligation to support community decisions with which he disagrees; who . . . views the political process as a power struggle to impose conformity rather than [as] a means of reconciling differences."

Dallas is filled with absolutists. But their abundance is not a new development in the city or in the state itself. Nearly ten years ago, Theodore H. White wrote that "within Texas, the machinery of government . . . has been captured by a nameless Third Party, obsessed with hate, fear and suspicion—one of whose central tenets is that 'If America is ever destroyed, it will be from within.'"

When White wrote that, he was concerned mostly with the oil people, Texas' famous "Big Rich." But the absolutists of Dallas today are by no means all "Big Rich." They are not even all little rich. Some of them (and some of the most vocal) are even poor by middle-class Dallas standards. This is what is surprising in Dallas. It is easy to understand why a group of men who came from bankruptcy to millions almost overnight would be stiffly resistant to change and to social progress. Old wealth is often liberal, as in the case of a Nelson Rockefeller; but new wealth is nearly always aggressively conservative, fearing that any change will suddenly take away what has so suddenly arrived. The oil men who supported Senator Joseph McCarthy and other right-wingers were behaving predictably in their resentment against a federal government which always seemed to be looking skeptically at such things as the oil depletion allowance. But in Dallas the absolute right includes barbers and baby-sitters as well as tycoons. It is an astonishing phenomenon when a single climate of opinion can so thoroughly blanket an American city, and it happens in Dallas, I think, because of factors that are peculiar to Dallas, others that are common to Texans, and some that are familiar in all of America.

Founded in 1841, Dallas is not even a half-century older than some of its elder citizens who still have a voice in community affairs. The city has reached a booming prosperity in very little time, and it has not done so by means of any single industry. Its leadership has pushed it in the direction of being a first class *service* city, in which white collars greatly outnumber blue collars. The result of this factor, coupled with the effect of Texas labor laws, has been that unions wield little power; their voice, loud and clear in most of the nation, is weak in Texas and almost nonexistent in Dallas.

In a blue-collar society, the boss is usually the enemy; in a white-collar society the boss is the point of closest orientation for his second-level associates, and often his influence reaches much further down into his organization. If the boss is conservative—as he nearly always is—then conservatism becomes a major factor in getting to be the boss. Quite often, on the second or third level, this conservatism may take on a more absolute quality than the boss himself may feel.

Americans are notoriously poor judges of stopping-points. If conservatism is good, then absolute conservatism is better; especially when nobody says it isn't. The boss himself is sometimes urged into moderation by the more moderate bankers who lend him money or the insurance men who build his buildings. On lower levels —as Robert Stoltz, the S. M. U. psychologist, has pointed out—the tendency is often for people to outdo each other rather than to moderate each other.

We begin, then, with a white-collar city oriented towards management. In Dallas, this situation is complicated by the suddenness of its prosperity and by the fact that this prosperity can be traced to the efforts of men working without the help of nature. The Citizens' Council, as I have said, often gives the impression that the city is being run from the City Club, rather than from City Hall. Management takes on much more glamor than it has in other American cities, but glamor does not mean wisdom, and glamor does not mean confidence.

It may be too early to expect wisdom from the leaders of Dallas; it seems to me certain that it is too early to expect confidence. The insecurity of the whole American people, thrown into world leadership very early in their country's existence, is reflected (and magnified, as are many things) in the insecurity of Dallas citizens. Insecurity is not easy to live with. Somehow, people must fight it. The most common weapons they choose for the fight are a defensive reaction to any kind of criticism, boastfulness, and a refusal to cope with contradiction, which must lead to confusion and back to insecurity.

Bill Johnson, now a writer and teacher at U. C. L. A., ran the *Time-Life* bureau in Dallas for a number of years. "I wrote pieces [about Dallas] all the time that I thought were very favorable," he said recently. "They were always resented. People always found something critical in them; they didn't balance the good things against the critical things. They only saw the critical ones. It had to be all good, or it was no good."

This is just as true in the spoken word. A pleasant conversation can turn unpleasant quickly if someone criticizes aspects of Dallas. When the Reverend William Holmes made his now famous remark about a report that Dallas school children had applauded upon hearing of the President's death, much of the criticism of Holmes was not on the basis of whether his statement was true or not; it was on the basis that he should not have said it, *even if it were true,* because it was bad public relations for Dallas.

The need for approval which causes this sensitivity to criticism goes further in Dallas than the need for respect; it is a need for popularity. Men try not only to be admired, but to be loved. In Dallas it is considerably easier to be popular in most circles if one proclaims oneself a conservative. I think this is one reason why one hears so little from the liberals of the city. It has been said that to be a liberal Democrat actually hurts a man's earning ability in Dallas, and in some businesses it is quite true.

But another reason the liberals are quiet is that they are like the conservatives; they, too, want to be popular. For example, if I should write a letter to the *Dallas News* in praise of Adlai Stevenson and the newspaper were to publish it, there would be numerous replies from the right wing condemning me. If I wrote a letter to the *News* praising Major General Edwin A. Walker, I might get some approving letters, but none disapproving. The liberals simply wouldn't bother with me, the moderate right wouldn't read my letter, and the far right would applaud. If I wrote a letter in praise of

Senator Barry Goldwater, the moderates and the extremists would both cheer me, and the liberals again would not bother. In Dallas these days, a man who wishes to be loved, admired, and on good terms with his boss and his second-level colleagues would be a Goldwater man.

It will be interesting to see what happens in November when President Johnson, the first Texas President, runs against the Republican nominee. The conflict between sound business practice and political philosophy should be well tested in Dallas.

Frontier days in Texas are not so very far in the past, and in the early days fighting out a living from the rough soil under the baking sun was a hard proposition. The man who could do it was a worker, a fighter, his own protector and dependent on no one. Challenged, he fought with his gun or his fists, and he fought the land, too, as he would an enemy. He was a man of action rather than of contemplation; he was an individualist, and he took great pride in victory—over the land and over other men. His life was made up of elemental facts, and fundamentalist preaching confirmed his conviction that things were either black or white.

Meanwhile, most of America has moved over the years towards a collectivist society. We act in groups. Politicians consider bloc votes. Authority and stature come from numbers and from unity of purpose among the numbers. As labor unions grew in strength they met their influence as groups; similarly, their counterparts in management and the professions found new power in lobbying as groups. Collectivism even gave women power. The theory of individualism, whether we wish to admit it or not, has been dying slowly through the century.

In Texas, still closer to the frontier, the individualist philosophy is by no means dead. The men who came from dugouts in Hico County and the swirling dust of the Panhandle are often still the leaders in today's Texas. When they are not, their sons are. And they have attracted admirers of individualism from other states. The man who acts, who fights, who resists trespass, who takes no orders from groups or from other men and who will not compromise—he is the frontier man, and he is still around in Dallas, and in Texas.

"AGGRESS: 1. To come forth and assert; 2. to come forth to destroy; 3. to come forth to defend against the encroachment of a right."

The third definition would describe the behavior of many Texans, but there are times when their attacks seem to fit the second definition before the conditions of the third have been established.

"In psychiatry," said Dr. Robert Glenn of Dallas, "the

word 'comfort' is often used. With Texans I never use it. I tell my patients that psychiatric treatment will be long and tough; very tough. They understand this. They would reject any concept of comfort."

A certain kinship with adversity does exist in Texas. Part of it may come from guilt. The oil business is a rough one, and more people have lost than won in it. Those who have won have always had one quality going for them in addition to courage and determination; they have had luck, and luck can bring on guilt feelings which may last for more than a generation. Texans are inclined sometimes to wonder whether they have really earned what they have.

"Out in Preston Hollow," a Dallas man said to me recently, "I see all these $30,000 houses, inhabited, a lot of times, by people whose parents earned a sixth of that in a year and worked like hell for that sixth. Whenever I have dinner with one of these families and I see the husband's eyes narrow—or sometimes the wife's—when some political thing comes up, I always wonder if it doesn't get back to guilt. The parents worked so hard for so little, and the sons worked so little—by their own frontier standards—for so much. Funny thing is, these sons really do work hard. They just can't convince themselves of it; not in comparison with the old days."

The visitor to Dallas is not likely to be particularly impressed or depressed by the existence of the wild-eyed right wing. Instead, what will dismay him is the lack of control over this element by the police, the press and other citizens. He will be shocked at a certain aura of respectability given to the far right. He will ask himself, perhaps, why people of this persuasion are not made to feel unwelcome in the community. Eventually he will understand that they are simple extensions, gone out of control, of many of the people he will see around him and with whom he will have lunch or dinner. He will sometimes even hear excuses made for gangster tactics. "They go too far," he will hear, "but I can't help sympathizing with their aims." If he challenges these aims, the visitor will begin to realize that he is talking to cement. Such people are too insecure to live with doubt.

5 | The compulsive
    right-wing woman

A couple of years ago in Dallas, I was lunching with a
friend. He is in his forties, a conservative, and holds a
very responsible position in the community. We had
lunched at the Dallas Club in the Republic Bank Building, and afterwards I walked him down to the bank
garage to get his car. When it pulled up, I noticed that
it carried a sticker reading IMPEACH EARL WARREN. This

was a fairly common car sticker around Dallas at the time, but I was amazed to see it on my friend's car, since his conservatism does not go to such lengths. I looked at him, and he obviously understood the expression on my face.

"It's my wife's car," he said wryly. "Mine's in the shop. I didn't have time to razor it off this morning. I don't think I had the nerve, either. It's not as bad as it might be. If she had her way, the sign would read HANG EARL WARREN. Thank God that's illegal."

In Dallas I know a number of men who do not discuss politics with their wives. The men themselves are conservative, but they are far outmatched by their women in absolutist thinking and in the projection of anger to cover up fears and anxiety. If the Texas male is insecure because his stature has come so quickly that he does not quite believe in it, his wife is more insecure.

(Retailers see this more clearly than most people because they come in contact with women, and lots of them, daily. Years ago, the *New Yorker* printed a cartoon showing a man and woman, practically barefoot, watching what is obviously the man's first gusher blow to the sky. "How late does Neiman-Marcus stay open?" the wife is saying.)

Women have a deep preoccupation with being "right," or at least in being "not wrong." Wearing the wrong hat or gloves with a suit is a disaster. Setting a table properly has such importance to so many women that department stores in America have great success with promotions for which leading community figures do the tables, sometimes with their own possessions, sometimes borrowing the stores'; and other women flock in to learn. This kind of insecurity exists also in Dallas women. Neiman-Marcus may be the only store in the world which set up a service specifically for insecure women. Of course, it wasn't called any such thing; it was given a woman's name. Its basic *raison d'être* was to give confidence to insecure women, and the person who ran it was chosen for her warmth and friendliness rather than for her fashion knowledge. She would advise women what to take to Chicago for a convention she was going to with her husband, what to wear to a tea, and how to cater a dinner for six to which her husband's boss was coming.

The quest for security and status shows up in woman's age-old search through yellowed documents for genealogical proof of her existence. Recognizing the difference between the kind of status bought by a full-length mink coat and another kind brought about by a confederate general in the family, these women join one of the dozens of old patriotic societies which exist all over America and especially in the South, the region of this country which has been valiantly defending its status since the Civil War.

The shifting class mobility of America is especially pronounced in Texas, where prosperity has come so quickly—sometimes overnight. In Dallas we see the country nurse who has moved to the city with her doctor husband and is suddenly living in a $125,000 house. The doctor has the practice of medicine with all its techniques to occupy him and to keep away confusion and doubt; the country nurse is concerned with all the things that *bring* confusion: how to decorate her house, how to entertain, what to wear, what to say and what not to say. Men have their business or professional competence to give them stature in a community. A woman must be competent in the very fields which often cause her the most worry. The husband is developing in a business which is not new to him. When he is successful, his wife has to develop, overnight, competence in a field which is completely new to her.

Since problems of insecurity often bring on anger and the desire to lash out, it is not surprising that in emotional matters (and in America, that would certainly include politics) women are often angrier than men. At the present time in this country, other factors make the lot of women even more difficult, especially a certain type of woman, the type who might end by wishing to place a sign reading HANG EARL WARREN on her car bumper.

Such a woman is over thirty-five, sometimes well

over. She does not have a job. Her children are gone from the household most of the time or for good. The husband is well off, sometimes very successful. (If he is poor, she will have too many problems maintaining her house to worry about her frustrations; if he is really rich, she can always hop around the world or engage herself in building a new house in Palm Springs or outside of Madrid. But if the husband is in between, his wife can have passed one point without reaching the other.)

The marriage has lasted fifteen or twenty years and, in Thurber's words, the magic has gone out of it. The successful husband is either actually consumed by his work and community affairs, or he pretends to be because he finds no interest in his relationship at home. Close contact between husband and wife has long since disintegrated. Their conversation is desultory. Common matters of interest can be disposed of quickly. Like other points of contact, the sexual relationship has either died entirely or comes alive rarely and without joy. There is no overt hostility in the household, but communication is feeble if it exists at all.

I know a good many women of this kind in Dallas and elsewhere, and at some point or other they say to themselves, "What am I here for? Who needs me? What should I do?"

This is the classic portrait of the disenfranchised woman in an America which won't even allow her to do the wash any more. From this kind of degradation, what are her outlets?

Some of these women turn to alcohol, perhaps the saddest solution of all. We have a growing number of women alcoholics in America, and the growth factor is accounted for mainly by the kind of woman I am talking about. Others get themselves involved in extramarital sex. They have an affair or sometimes a succession of affairs and in the end succeed in degrading themselves further in their own eyes. Still others turn into compulsive shoppers, going daily to a store where they know they will be recognized and treated with deference. Quite a few stores would have a tough time making ends meet if it were not for these women.

But many of the so-called jobless women band together in groups of one kind or another. Dr. Arthur Clinco, a Los Angeles psychiatrist who has studied many such women, says, "The woman you are talking about is seeking attention. . . . Often she will join groups of other bored women. They work on civic projects, put on charity balls, or even simply play cards all day. They get involved in public affairs, engage speakers, go on campaigns. They're saying to men, 'Anything you can do, I can do better.' There's great competitive force within them. They're mad at men, the world and themselves. Outwardly and inwardly they are angry and frustrated. But if you ask them whether they are willing to get involved in something that is demanding and spend enough time and energy at it to become really proficient, the answer is no.

"So we have the hobby-of-the-month club, always pursued in groups. One month it's painting, the next it's doing mosaic tables, each woman hoping someone else has the answer. Each looking for instant status, instant culture, instant attainment."

But sometimes, these harmless and often valuable pursuits, do not, by themselves, solve the woman's problem. "Any time a person's sense of existence is challenged," says Dr. Robert Glenn, social psychiatrist at Southwestern Medical School in Dallas, "anger, even rage, results."

This may be the reason that, for at least the past fifteen years, still another extreme outlet for such women has made itself felt in the life of the country, and especially in certain parts of it, including Texas. This is the outlet of the angry right wing. At manifestations in Dallas over these years, women have been, on the whole, more obviously numerous, more vocal, more absolute and sometimes even more physical than men. In controversies involving what pictures not to hang in the

Museum of Fine Arts, what speakers not to engage for colleges, schools, or even the Council of World Affairs, what textbooks not to use in the schools and what matters preachers may not undertake to discuss, right-wing women have consistently outdone their men. (Most such groups are *against* things; they are *for* God and country but *against* specifics.) Most of the people who nearly mobbed Senator Lyndon Johnson and his wife in Dallas in 1960 were women. More than half the placard carriers during Ambassador Adlai Stevenson's visit to Dallas were women, and one of them struck him. Prior to President Kennedy's arrival, the right-wing literature being circulated was handed out mainly by women. And in Dallas it is popularly thought that right-wing Republican Congressman Bruce Alger might well be out of office if it weren't for the women's vote.

The fury of women is not something which has been underestimated through the ages. Civilization has a number of proverbs on the matter. In earlier days, however, female fury usually manifested itself in the sex war with men. Since the suffragettes, women have been turning it on ideological concepts, and in recent years this rage has been emanating from the far right and has been directed towards anything, literally anything, not equally far right. (I do not wish to state that by turning to politics, women have separated themselves from the war between the sexes. The chances are, in fact, that political extremism is just another facet of women's approach to the same old battle.) Whatever it is, this extremism must be examined. In Texas as well as other parts of America, it carries weight both in terms of votes and violence.

This feminine (if that is the word) radicalism probably came to the attention of many Americans during the heyday of Senator Joseph McCarthy, whose fan mail from women must have interested Metro-Goldwyn-Mayer. In those days, McCarthy was an inevitable subject of conversation over the soup or the roast beef at dinner parties, at least in Texas. For a while, I remember, violent arguments came about. The Senator had a good deal of financial support from Texas, as well as moral backing, and the money was coming from some of the famous Big Rich. Since money is often equated with wisdom in Texas, McCarthy had some good names, such as Hugh Roy Cullen, Clint Murchison and even Governor Allan Shivers going for him. In addition to this, he spoke an understandable language. He spoke of internal fear, a preoccupying subject with Texans. You were either for him or against him. And so, at dinner, the Senator provoked violent controversy, at least for a time. Then suddenly his enemies shut up. When they did, his backers shut up.

I don't speak for other enemies of McCarthyism, but I know the exact moment when I shut up. A handsome woman of fifty sitting across the table from me said, "Why don't you go back where you came from—you and all your Yankee pinko friends?" I had known her three or four years and I liked her, but now her eyes were narrow and dead, and her mouth was twisted. Her husband tried to remonstrate, the host changed the subject, and I had seen the kind of face we all have seen since then: the contorted face of hatred which has been caught by the television cameras on the women of Birmingham, New Orleans and Little Rock.

Other people must have had the same experience, or something close to it. Until after the Army-McCarthy hearings, the Senator was often discussed in Dallas, but seldom in argument. Liberals discussed him and agreed; conservatives discussed him and agreed. When both sides were present, he did not very often come up for discussion. It was sad that a symbol of healthy disunity could turn into the symbol of unity, group against group. After the Army hearings his support seemed to evaporate; he was discussed almost not at all.

Whatever else McCarthy was, he was a man of action. Under questioning, against contradictory evidence, he retaliated by instinct, not by plan. In this sense he had something in common with Major General Edwin A. Walker, who seems to have been the nominal head of the far right in Dallas ever since he selected the city as his home. Having been relieved of his command in Germany for trying to indoctrinate American troops with his political philosophy, Walker came to live in Dallas because it seemed to offer a political climate in which he would be welcome—and he was. At first the local press carried his various pronouncements, and he became something of a rallying point among the ultra-conservatives of Dallas. For most people, however, the disenchantment came quickly. Walker is a hazy speaker as well as a hazy thinker. He is no spellbinder of the Father Coughlin or Gerald L. K. Smith type. The press grew disillusioned quickly, if indeed it had ever had any illusions.

One day two ex-wire service newspapermen went to see Walker at his request. What he had in mind, it developed, was to build a news service like the Associated Press; the difference would be that his service would carry only articles that were friendly to General Walker and his cohorts and would send news only to those American papers who believed as he did.

After a moment of stunned amazement, one of the newsmen asked him if he had considered that such an enterprise might cost a hundred million dollars, and that few people would use it even then.

The general, apparently, had not considered any such thing. According to the newsmen, he drew a line down his desk and asked them which side they stood on. It was not possible, he said, to straddle the fence. As an answer, the newsmen left.

Walker may also have hoped to be supported by some of the big, ultra-conservative money in Texas. But Texans like a winner. McCarthy lost his Texas support when Joseph Welch, special counsel for the Army, disgraced him in front of millions on television. Walker lost his chance for big money when he ran sixth in a field of six in the gubernatorial elections in 1962.

Yet he still has support in Dallas, and it seems to come mainly from women.

In spite of the fact that most Dallas conservatives do not take him seriously, Walker was the principal speaker on U. S. Day, a right-wing demonstration held just before UN Day, and he managed to fan his audience— much of it female—into a suitable frenzy against Ambassador Adlai Stevenson, who was to arrive the next day. And when the general underwent psychiatric examination to determine whether he should stand trial for his part in the Mississippi rioting, Dr. Robert Stubblefield, head of the psychiatric division of the University of Texas Medical School in Dallas, examined him.

"I had stacks of mail," Stubblefield said recently. "The tenor of most of it was, 'How can you examine this great hero?' The great majority of the letters were from women."

Congressman Bruce Alger seems to inspire this same kind of devotion among women. Criticizing Alger is dangerous in certain Dallas groups. He is a good-looking sort of fellow and obviously has sex appeal. But the emotional backing he has from a good many women is more deeply rooted than a politician's sex appeal can produce.

A public relations man who fought Alger in the last election explained it this way: "He acts. He strikes out. He's always fighting something the government's going to do or has done. To these gals, he's not just a politician supposed to represent a district. He's some kind of knight, standing up there in Washington with his sword and his white horse, defending honor and chastity against all the villains. The villains in this case are other Congressmen, Senators and even the President. Or maybe the main villain is the twentieth century, I don't know. Anyway, he's got the gals behind him, and they make him hard to beat."

The Texas right-wing woman became celebrated in 1953 when the *Houston Post* published a long series of articles on an organization called the Minute Women. Written by the late Ralph O'Leary, the series was later picked up by *Time* and other national magazines. It was a courageous series for the *Post* to publish, since most of the women O'Leary was writing about were actual or potential customers of the newspaper's advertisers. While the national comment was probably advantageous to the newspaper, local protests were certainly damaging.

The Minute Women were founded by a woman named Mrs. Suzanne Silvercruys Stevenson on September 22, 1949, in Connecticut. Mrs. Stevenson, Belgian-born, was a sculptress, and at the time her brother was Ambassador from Belgium to the United States. The announced purposes of her new organization were:

1. Actively to fight Communism in every form
2. To demand the removal of Socialism and Communism in our federal and state governments and in our educational system
3. To demand the teaching of our American heritage in schools and colleges

The dues were light but they enabled Mrs. Stevenson to publish a newsletter and to issue lapel pins for new members. On the pins was written the slogan "Guarding the Land We Love."

Mrs. Stevenson's organization was ingenious. For example, there was no constitution and there were no by-laws. No parliamentary procedure existed at meetings. Officers were not elected. National, local and policy council officials were all appointed. The reason she gave for this somewhat arbitrary organizational procedure was that it enabled the Minute Women to avoid subversive infiltration. O'Leary's comment was: "Such goings-on can undoubtedly be effective in guarding against subversives. Unfortunately, democracy is just as effectively barred from the organization."

Another interesting point of organization was that there were no letters, no postcards and almost nothing in writing with the exception of the newsletter. Minute Women were supposed to tell each other about meetings or other issues by the pyramid system. Each woman, in other words, had to call five other women—later ten —each of whom was to call five more women, and so forth—the theory of the chain letter. In this way, meetings could be called at a moment's notice. Parenthetically, it is interesting to note that some women belonged to the organization for months without knowing that friends or enemies also belonged.

In 1953, the *Post* roughly estimated that there were a thousand women in Houston who belonged to the organization. It was estimated by news reporters in Dallas —though neither Dallas newspaper followed the *Houston Post's* lead in publicizing the group—that about the same number of women belonged to the group in Dallas. Membership in both cities came largely from the top residential districts and from the upper-middle to upper income group. (Hairdressers, dressmakers and others whose income was dependent on wealthy women, were also members.) A somewhat disproportionate share of the members came from the ranks of doctors' wives (presumably worried about socialized medicine), from the wives of oil executives of one kind or another (presumably worried about the depletion allowance), and from old patriotic organizations for women (presumably worried about what to do with themselves).

As can be seen by some of their unusual by-laws (or lack of them) the Minute Women were urged by Mrs. Stevenson never to present the appearance of an organization. Instead, they were encouraged to write letters, to picket and to register protests as individuals. The theory was that five hundred letters to a Congressman, newspaper, church, college or school board would have far more impact as individual letters than they would if they arrived as part of an organizational project. In today's world pressure groups are common, but five hundred individuals are always impressive.

To this moment, it is impossible to find out exactly how many Minute Women there were and are in Houston and in Dallas. The *Post* articles subdued them in Houston and may have reduced their number. (Since no such articles appeared in the Dallas press, the Minute Women continued as before, except when their numbers split off to join groups like the John Birch Society, the National Indignation Committee or the Friends of General Walker.) Whatever their number is, it is not inconsiderable. Why? In support of Dr. Clinco's theory that frustrated women seek instant attainment, it should at least be said that joining the Minute Women or the John Birch Society is a lot easier than the long, hard job of raising money for an orchestra or a museum, though a few women do both and win a quasi-respectability in the total community instead of just the right wing section of it.

The psychology of the individual woman who joins the organized radical right is explained thus by Dr. Clinco: he draws a rectangle and inside it writes four words in ascending order: resentment, anger, fury, blind rage. What is resentment in one woman may be fury in another. Nevertheless, conscience often produces in a woman the perfection complex, as in the familiar pattern of the woman whose house must always be in perfect order, perfect taste. If it is not, or someone *suggests* that it is not, one of the four reactions in Dr. Clinco's rectangle will result. Such a woman's mind, Dr. Clinco feels, will be politically as organized, as carefully compartmentalized, as it is in other ways. Issues are black or white. When the compartments are threatened, the resentment rectangle ensues.

We have then the concept of directed political anger filling up the vacuum in these women's lives; anger becomes a part of American leisure. And we have threatened confusion bringing on violent reaction. Agreeing with these notions, George R. Bach, director of the Institute of Group Psychotherapy in Beverly Hills, puts it in another way.

"Aggression in American women may be dormant," he says, "but it is never tamed. Territorial aggression in her brings on the reaction of the snake or the fish or any animal which, when cornered, fights. Down in Texas, this feeling of trespassing has been tremendously important. You govern your own affairs, you say. Then that guy comes along with his popularity and his handsomeness and so forth to confuse you. One reason these women hated Kennedy so much was that they were confused by him."

Bach also points out that women groping for status and achievement will join extremist movements, such as the angry right wing, only if the atmosphere around them supports these causes. "I never hit my wife when I'm in Paris," he said recently. "But in Berlin, whack! In Paris she might crack me; but never in Berlin."

As one of the country's leading experts on aggressions Bach has studied literally thousands of American marriages. (He feels, among other things, that quarreling between married people is not only inevitable but desirable when the quarrels are planned constructively.) In terms of these studies, he remarked: "It's interesting that in seven out of ten harmonious marriages, the couples jointly hate something outside their marriage. This can be a child—which is the most tragic—or the Jews, the United Nations, or whatever. These aggressions are directed outside rather than into their marriage. The husband and wife are civil to each other."

Within a large group in Dallas, the status of a woman who is extreme right-wing, anti-Administration, anti-United Nations, anti-public welfare (when it is dependent on government aid) is predictably high. If she thinks Madame Nhu is the greatest woman in the world (as several score of women who followed her around Dallas one day apparently did), her status remains high. If she engages a leading Bircher to speak to her luncheon club and then boos or pickets a liberal when he is speaking somewhere else, her status is perhaps even higher; she is not only fashionably right-wing, but energetic. (But if she spits on someone, or hits someone else over the head, her status drops because of conduct unbecoming to a lady.) The fact that thousands of other Dallas citizens consider her something of a nut doesn't bother her. She sees few or none of them face to face. They are the vague, uncounted, black side of her world; she and her friends, whom she sees daily, are the countable, comfortable, white.

The fact that right-wing women are more dogmatic and often more outspoken than their men should not really be surprising. Over the course of history scientists, philosophers and poets have found that women, especially women acting in groups, are more dogmatic and fiercer about nearly everything than men.

William Butler Yeats described it in *Dramatis Personae:* "To women, opinions become as their children or their sweethearts, and the greater their emotional capacity, the more do they forget all other things. They grow cruel, as if in defense of lover or child, and this is done 'for something other than human life.' At last, the opinion is so much identified with their natures that it seems a part of their flesh, becomes stone and passes out of life."

Elizabeth Mann Borgese, in her *Ascent of Woman,* points out that women as individuals are not more suggestible than men. In groups, she says, the story is different: "If, nevertheless, women at all times and in the most different sets of circumstances, have more easily fallen prey to collective frenzy or shared 'epidemic emotions,' this may be explained by the affinity of their minds and the crowds' mind. The group force acts more directly on women than on men; or on the average—and in dealing with a group force, we are by definition concerned only with the average—the group force acts on a larger section of the mind in the case of women . . ."

Mrs. Borgese's book is an attempt to draw a parallel between the rise of a collectivist society during the last century—as opposed to a prior history dedicated to the emancipation of the individual—and the ascent of woman. She traces the deep-seated affinity between the feminine collective through the fields of anthropology, biology and psychology among others, and finds that woman in a collectivist society has become far more important than she was in individualist ones.

"It has been observed time and again that women made good Nazis," she writes. "They frequently put party interests ahead of the family as can be seen from the number of divorces granted on the grounds that the plaintiff—wife—was a Nazi and that the defendant husband did not live up (or down) to her standards. The attractiveness of Nazism for women has been ascribed particularly to the fact that it gave them the feeling of 'belonging.' It increased their group or community feeling . . ."

All these characteristics have shown up in the role women have played in the development of the Radical Right in America. Seymour Martin Lipset, professor of sociology and director of the Institute of International Studies of the University of California at Berkeley, has said:

"It is worth noting that existing evidence suggests that there is a substantial difference in the reactions of men and women to the radical right. Women are much more likely to support repressive measures against Communists and other deviate groups than are men, as measured by poll responses, and many of the organizations which are active in local struggles to intimidate school and library boards are women's groups. In part, this difference may be related to the fact that women are more explicitly concerned with family status in the community than are men in the American culture, and hence may react more than the men do to status anxieties or frustrations. The organizations of old family Americans which were concerned with claiming status from the past are predominantly female. Hence, if the thesis that status concerns are related to rightist extremism and bigotry is valid, one would expect to find more women than men affected by it."

Massing all these factors together in Dallas, the city would seem obviously receptive to extreme right-wing women, and so it has proved to be. The ultra-conservative climate of the city, as reflected in the statements of its leaders and opinion voiced in the public media, provides the necessary respectability. There are as many frustrated women without a job in Dallas as anywhere else, and perhaps more. The right wing provides instant status, instant attainment for such women. The group psychology of the right wing is as strong in Dallas as anywhere, and in Dallas the group is larger and publicly unopposed except in minor skirmishes—never in full-scale war. The moral cause, though highly dubious in

124 | DALLAS PUBLIC AND PRIVATE

actuality, is *apparently* patriotic and on the side of God and the angels. And the fear psychology of so many Texas men who think the federal government is trying to take property away from them takes hold of their wives as well, and in their wives it becomes more intense.

The key to moderating immoderate women is probably not to be found in men. In Hitler's Germany, we have noted, women divorced men for not living up to their own immoderation. In Dallas a man whose wife had committed a particularly outrageous act on behalf of the right wing confided to a friend that he had lost considerable business as a result. The friend asked why he could not control his wife. "Control her?" the man answered. "Hell, I can't even *talk* to her."

The right-wing women's groups will be quieter (and eventually will disband) only when their actions and their philosophies are no longer respectable in the total community and when the community makes this known. In any choice between absolutism and status among women, status will usually win. After all, there are always the mosaic tables.

Meanwhile, it has occurred to many Dallas people to wonder what would happen if Chief Justice Earl Warren should have to visit Dallas; even after all that has happened, the thought is chilling.

6 | Inside and outside the law

Americans are the most violent and lawless people among all civilized nations, but few citizens realize it. In Los Angeles recently, Dr. Arthur Clinco was musing about some incidents of violence which have taken place in the United States.

"There are," he said, "two myths Americans believe. The first is that we are a peace-loving people. Nothing in our history indicates this. When we haven't been fighting other people, we've always been fighting and doing violence among ourselves.

"The second is that human beings have made progress in controlling their emotions. In two thousand years, much progress has been made in other fields but we've gained no ground in emotional control. In fact, our emotions are probably less disciplined today than they've ever been."

Americans have more laws than any other people and we break them all. J. Edgar Hoover points out that crime costs the United States more than $20,000,000,000 a year and this price, like others, is rising. Americans are the world's champion murderers—and world champions in every form of violent crime. No state supports this leadership with more robust enthusiasm than Texas. In *The Super-Americans,* John Bainbridge's excellent study of the Texas millionaires, he writes:

"Nothing indicates the low state of the demand for law in Texas more clearly than the figures on homicides. Of all crimes, murder, as W. H. Auden has pointed out, is alone in being an offense against both God and society. Murder is therefore *the* crime—the main event in the criminal sweepstakes. Here, Texas wins handily. In each of the last four years, more murders have been committed in Texas than in any other state, regardless of population. In 1959, a thousand and ninety-four persons were shot, stabbed, clubbed or otherwise snuffed out in Texas; that was more than twice as many as in New York which has seven million more people. Put another way, more people killed other people in Texas in 1959 than in all the New England states together plus Iowa, Kansas, Minnesota, Nebraska, North Dakota, South Dakota, Montana and Utah. To make an international comparison: every year there are more murders in Dallas alone than in England, which has approximately forty-five million more people, and every year Houston has more murders than Dallas. Any way you look at it, Texas is tops in murder."

Since 1959 the murder rate has continued to rise. Last year Dallas had about a 10 per cent increase in homicides, bringing the 1963 total to 114, including those of November 22 and 24. Oddly enough, none of these Dallas murders was associated with any organized and powerful underworld. Battles between gangsters which cost many lives and add to the murder figures in other cities have not been a factor in Dallas since the early fifties. Organized crime of all sorts is at a minimum in Dallas now. No scandal involving graft or corruption has touched the Dallas police force. In other words, the 5 per cent increase in the total number of major crimes and the 10 per cent jump in murders have been accomplished entirely by amateurs.

This is a logical consequence of such a situation, according to Dr. George Bach. He says, "Whenever you have programmed nonviolence and nonaggression in a city—as you have in Dallas and as there is in other cities —you always have increases in unpredictable and unexpected aggression. You have individualized violence. It is a corollary."

Dallas has an elaborate history of crime and violence, both amateur and professional.

In the late twenties and early thirties, the late Ben Whittaker ran the gambling in Dallas. He worked in partnership with Earl Dalton and occasionally with Benny Binion, an illiterate man known as "Benny the Cowboy." In those days the police raided the games about once a week. Fines were paid, and the gambling closed for the day and reopened in the morning. It was what amounted to a licensing fee of about $100 a week.

Murders usually came about when some outsider tried to muscle in on the profitable businesses of bookmaking, dice games, policy rackets, etc. A newcomer named Sam Murray tried to do this and was killed when he walked into a "bank." (A "banker" is a man who takes care of things at city hall.) The murder was ascribed to a member of Binion's gang.

Another man mixed up in the gambling operations was Herbert Noble, who was at first a friend and colleague of Binion. Later, however, a man who worked for Binion killed a friend of Noble. Not long afterward, the murderer himself was shot in the driveway of his home. The bad blood between Binion and Noble probably began then, but nothing happened for years. They were both too successful. By the time the Texas Centennial opened in 1936, you could find a dice game or a book-maker up almost any stairway in the city of Dallas. This went on until after World War II.

In the mid-forties, the national crime syndicate tried to take over the very profitable Dallas operation. A man named Paul Jones arrived in town to lay the ground-work for this, but he made a mess of things by attempt-ing to bribe Sheriff Steve Guthrie. He was sent to jail. Later two or three other men arrived from Chicago, but they were met at the plane and deported by the new sheriff, Bill Decker, and by Detective Captain Will Fritz, who is familiar now to millions of television view-ers as the chief Dallas investigator of the murder of President John F. Kennedy and of Lee Harvey Oswald.

The city had not worried too greatly about its gam-bling operations so long as they were under the banner of Whittaker. He was rather liked in the community and he ran a "gentle game." He was not fond of homicide. When it looked as though gang warfare might result from the national syndicate's interest in Dallas, he cut up his Dallas business and got rid of it.

Will Wilson was elected district attorney of Dallas County in 1956. A North Dallas boy, he was elected principally by The Establishment areas and was told to clean out the gambling before any open warfare broke out. Wilson did his job. Before he was through he had every major gambler in the city out of business and most of them out of the city. Binion himself went to Las Vegas and eventually to Leavenworth for income tax evasion.

The gambling interests in Dallas were separated by the usual unwritten law from the flesh business. Prostitution was run by a young man with the unlikely name of Lois Green. Most of the time the Green gang concentrated on keeping the county's prostitution a healthy and active business, but occasionally they branched off into burglary and hijacking. Green himself was the son of a prostitute and grew up in a whorehouse at which his mother finally became the madam. Sent off into the world to carry on the family standards, Green did well.

At one time there were no professional prostitutes in Dallas who were independent of Lois Green. He worked with his counterparts in Louisiana and Oklahoma in setting up a circuit of tourist courts and hotels and running the girls from one to another, usually for not more than two weeks in a single town. The girls who held out percentages were either never seen again or were pulled out of the various lakes in the vicinity.

There was some bad blood between Green and Herbert Noble (who seems to have had trouble getting along with *anyone*) and when Green was shot and killed in the doorway of the old Sky Club in Oak Cliff, it was popularly thought that Noble's friends might have had something to do with it. No one was ever charged with the murder.

With their leader gone, Green's gang broke up. Like other crimes in Dallas, prostitution is now on a far less organized basis than it used to be.

In the late forties and fifties, a peculiarity of the city's downtown night life was the "mechanized girl." A man could walk down Commerce Street from the Chamber of Commerce Building to the Adolphus Hotel, circle around to Main Street and then back down past Webb's Waffle Shop to Commerce again, and be picked up four or five times by young women in cars.

These girls were not necessarily prostitutes as much as they were pickpockets; some of them were both. The queen of this group was the late and much lamented Maude Lynch who was arrested nearly eight hundred times during her long and profitable career. She wore diamonds and a fur coat and drove Cadillacs. Occasionally, she would slow up behind some fellow walking down the street and simply ask him if he wanted to go for a ride. More often, around the convention headquarters of the Adolphus and Baker hotels, she would go up to a likely prospect, grab his arm and say, "John, how are you?"

The surprised gentleman, whose name was Tim (or Bob or Dick), would then be treated to Maude's spiel: "Oh, my dear, please forgive me. I thought you were John Harris, a friend of my husband. My husband is a doctor and he's off attending a medical meeting. I thought perhaps we might have dinner. . . ."

Once Maude got him in the car, he would nearly always leave it penniless. Maude didn't bother with hotels or motels. She just drove her men to a sort of lover's leap. There she would neck with them for a while while she removed the currency from their wallets.

Not many of Maude's gentlemen friends did much complaining for obvious reasons. When one of them did, Maude occasionally gave the money back if she was feeling charitable, and sometimes didn't when she wasn't. But Maude had her friends around city hall. One man from New York was determined to prosecute her and flew to Dallas four separate times to present his case in court. Each time the case was postponed and eventually he gave up in disgust, to Maude's great delight. When she died a few years ago, the "mechanized girls" seemed to become discouraged at the loss of their leader. Today there is almost no open soliciting in Dallas. That does not mean that call girls can't be persuaded to join a party, but on the streets of downtown Dallas it would be highly unusual for a visitor to be accosted by a professional.

Until the end of the gambling era and the break up of the Green gang, organized crime had quite a day in Dallas. Lois Green was only thirty-four years old when he was shot on Christmas Eve, but he had been arrested thirty-five times for major crimes and he was wanted in four states. His gang members had served time in some twenty-six states; eventually, sixteen of them were murdered by their own colleagues.

The extraordinary murder story of the period, however, was the continued attempt by somebody over a period of years to kill Herbert Noble. Noble, as I have said, seemed to have a good deal of trouble in getting along with his friends and his competitors. While it was popularly supposed that Binion or his friends were out to kill him, no one has ever proved it. Nine separate attempts were made to kill Noble. One of them, a bomb placed in his automobile, killed his wife by mistake. When she started the car, it blew her hundreds of yards around the Oak Cliff neighborhood in which they lived.

Noble had great physical courage. At one time, being a pilot, he planned to bomb Binion in Las Vegas and had actually attached some bomb racks to his plane when a police acquaintance talked him out of it.

But he was never really the same after his wife's death. He began drinking and taking pills. Some of his acquaintances feel that the only reason he didn't take his own life was because he was so sure that somebody else would, and that out of pride he wanted to delay this as long as he could and perhaps take somebody with him.

At last, on August 7, 1951, at 11:35 A.M., the long war against Herbert Noble ended. A bomb placed beside his mailbox at a farm he owned near Dallas went off when he reached into the box. It was the end to one of the most extraordinary stories of dedicated assassination attempts in our country. It was also the end of the era of professional crime in Dallas.

"In this town, I'd rather any day defend a man accused of murder than one accused of drunken driving," Fred Bruner said to me. Bruner, a former assistant district attorney, is one of the top defense lawyers in Dallas. He was perfectly serious. In Dallas, driving while intoxicated carries some stiff penalties. The minimum punishment for a first offense is three days in jail, a fine of $50 and the suspension of the driver's license for six months. For a second offense, and even for some first offenses, the penalties can go way up.

Murder is rather lightly regarded by comparison.

There have been years when out of 1,200 or 1,300 murders in Texas, only three or four people went to the electric chair. Grand juries return almost as many no bills as true bills in the case of murder. A man can buy a gun in Texas with no difficulty. No law says he can't, and as a result a good many Texans own guns, though they do not normally wear them around town, contrary to press reports. When a murder case does come to trial, some of the courts are so overcrowded in Dallas that it may be weeks, months or even years before the actual trial gets under way. By that time, witnesses have disappeared or are dead and the prosecution's case is often immeasurably weakened.

It is also true that under Texas law juries not only decide on the merits of the case—that is to say, whether a man is guilty or innocent—but also on the penalty. This has resulted in some astonishing contrasts of sentencings. Murderers are often given five-year suspended sentences or less; but Candy Barr, the well-known stripper, was given fifteen years for possession of marijuana, a conviction that in other courts has often brought sentences of something like six months, suspended.

One could come to the conclusion that it is easy to commit murder in Dallas, that it is easy to be defended well and that the chances are pretty good to get away with a light sentence or no sentence at all.

For one thing, there is still an element of frontier justice in the deliberations of Texas juries. It is a land not
so long removed from a time when arguments and disputes were settled privately, and I suspect that in the
minds of many Texans there is still a sneaking admiration for the man (or woman) who takes matters into his
own hands. This is the famous "Code of the West." Each
man under the code is his own defender and his own
protector against transgressions, whatever these may be.
A huge mural in the Dallas County courthouse depicts
Judge Roy Bean, "the law west of the Pecos," and a man
given to dispensing folk justice. To the 1960s, his like-
ness and his spirit live on in Dallas. There is a statute in
Texas law that husbands are permitted to shoot other
men if the husband has reason to believe that "the other
man is committing adultery, has just committed adultery
or is about to commit adultery on his wife." This has
given hundreds of defense lawyers a quick and easy way
to pick up their fees. Self-defense and justifiable homicide, our leading defense arguments, are quite accept-
able to most juries. Temporary insanity is also used with
success. This, of course, allows a man who has, so to
speak, "gone insane" just long enough to commit murder, to walk around in the midst of the citizenry until
something irks him enough to "go insane" again. Women
who commit murder are especially easy to defend—
much easier than men, according to Houston's Percy

Foreman, one of the most colorful defense lawyers in the state. One understands Mr. Foreman's optimism about defending women when one notes that in a single year he defended thirteen women against the charge of murdering their husbands and stumbled only once; one woman got a five-year suspended sentence. All the others were acquitted.

Another aspect of the justice wheel is that in Texas, as in the South generally, there has been historically a double standard racially in terms of murder. If a white man murders a white man, he will be tried, he may be convicted, and the newspapers will carry stories on the case. If a Negro murders a white man, he will certainly be tried, usually convicted and quite often executed. If a Negro murders another Negro, he is likely not even to be tried, and there will be little publicity. If he is tried, he will usually get off with a light sentence or none at all.

This has not only contributed to the crime rate among low-income Negroes, but has been an important factor in the complexity of the entire problem of civil rights and integration. In Dallas it may be changing. Whenever the police can amass enough evidence and the district attorney thinks he has a good enough case, Negroes will be tried these days for the murder of other Negroes. One man not long ago got the death penalty, which would have been unheard-of a few years ago. Still, the general attitude involving crimes of violence in low-income Negro and Mexican settlements is a shrug of the shoulders. In the large cities, police departments are too under-manned properly to defend and protect the white citizenry. Whatever their convictions, they haven't the manpower to provide the same fairness in a cabin murder in South Dallas or a knifing in Little Mexico.

Some kind of fundamentalism may also enter into the deliberations of Texas juries. Prostitutes, dope addicts other people considered "sinful" often get rough sentences, much rougher than murderers. A Dallas defense attorney, after the extraordinary fifteen-year sentence given to stripteaser Candy Barr (for possession of narcotics), told me, "There were eleven men and one woman on that jury. All those men went home to their wives and said, 'Well, look at us, Ma; look what we did to that sinful creature, barin' her flesh and all that.' They were showing the world they were in favor of God and heaven and sending to eternal fire a girl who violated their sense of morality."

Although Dallas, along with the rest of Texas, seems to show a high incidence of murder, it is not in other respects a particularly lawless city. For instance, the latest crime figures from the Federal Bureau of Investigation would indicate that the city ranks twenty-fifth nationally in forceable rape, twenty-eighth in robbery, fourteenth in aggravated assault, seventeenth in burglary, forty-eighth in larceny over $50 and eighteenth in auto theft.

In some ways, the city is so law-abiding it isn't much fun—as thousands of conventioneers have pointed out. The Texas liquor laws make it impossible for a visitor to buy a mixed drink. Instead he must buy a bottle, which he can then bring into a night club or a bar, where he will be served a set-up that will cost him anywhere between fifty cents and seventy-five cents. These prices for a glass of water have irritated visitors but the alternative is to buy beer or wine which can be sold legally across a bar or in a night club. The inability to serve a decent mixed drink at a fair price has turned the city's public night clubs into rather glum places, usually featuring striptease artists. In addition, no liquor may be imbibed anywhere publicly after midnight on weekdays and after one o'clock Sunday mornings.

"I am forty-five years old and the father of two boys in college," a visiting lawyer once said. "It seems to me that I'm old enough to know what time I should go to bed. But in Dallas you tell me."

In Dallas the police and the state Liquor Control Board do indeed tell visitors what time to go to bed, and emphatically. Any public or private club serving liquor after hours runs the risk of a raid. When it is raided, everybody goes to jail, including the guests, until they pay their fines and are released. Prior to a professional football game between the New York Giants and the Dallas Cowboys, some of the New York sportswriters were sitting around the University Club, enjoying some Texas hospitality. The gathering became convivial and extended past the club's usual closing hours. It was raided and the visiting newsmen were packed off to jail to pay their fines. The kindest word any of them had to say about Dallas hospitality was "bush league."

The police and the Liquor Control Board have always been exceedingly careful with regard to public places, but for years the private clubs of Dallas operated more or less without interference. Festive evenings at the University Club, the Cipango Club, the Club 3525 and others often lasted until dawn. Many of the performers who were playing publicly at the Century Room of the Adolphus or at the Empire Room of the Statler Hilton would walk on down the street to the University Club and go through their acts all over again for no fee. As a result, the tiny spot became a famous landmark for a visiting celebrity, who could usually find a local member to get him in. Clubs like the University Club had the reputation among the authorities of being run honestly; of giving a fair drink for a fair dollar and of keeping out nonmembers, unless accompanied by members. For these reasons, the habit of staying open a bit late was overlooked.

The change occurred largely because of Club 3525,

which was located in the most fashionable apartment building on Turtle Creek Boulevard. The residents of the apartment house were mostly elderly people who had sold their big homes to retire to a less troublesome form of living offered by the apartment. Unfortunately the club, which was on the ground floor of the apartment building, became unsuitably lively for these tenants. Their irritation came to a head when, one night, a club member wandered up to one of the floors of the apartment house, hoping that he might run into somebody he knew, and stretched out in the hallway for a short nap. The next morning two elderly and very dignified Dallas women nearly tripped over him as they left their apartment.

This was too much, and the club began to be raided so regularly it finally went out of business. Since it was located in The Establishment area, the other clubs were warned to close up promptly or suffer the same fate. They did, and now even the Dallas residents are sent to bed at midnight.

How much this fatherly benevolence costs the city in terms of visitors' dollars is hard to estimate. Hotel, restaurant and retail store executives estimate that it is in the millions. Dallas has good convention facilities of every kind. The city is hospitable and pleasant to its visitors. Unfortunately, it has a tendency, also, to bore them. Conventioneers historically have applauded the presence around them of a little healthy sin and in this Dallas is sadly lacking.

No other institution of the city has come in for the ruthless criticism that the Dallas police got after the murder of Lee Harvey Oswald. It was inconceivable to the world that the most important prisoner of the century could be shot in a Dallas jail. It was also inconceivable to some people that Officer Tippit had to die before Oswald was apprehended.

In considering these two matters, it should be remembered that the police chief in Dallas is not elected, but appointed. He is responsible to the city manager, who is responsible to the City Council. The council is not responsible, officially, to anyone, but historically it has listened with high interest to what the Citizens' Council has had to say. In other words, Police Chief Jesse Curry is not entirely his own boss, any more than other Dallas police chiefs have been.

Like everything else in Dallas, the police force is management-oriented. "I used to be surprised," said Holland McCombs, who does a great deal of editorial work for *Life* magazine in Dallas, "by the number of policemen Exchange Park could get out to supervise parking in a new plant. In my job, I had to know that a good deal of violent crime was taking place in the city, and here were all these officers steering people into the right parking places. I remember that I always used to think that the Dallas police were tougher on jaywalkers than on murderers—to coin a phrase." (Jaywalking carries a $5 fine in Dallas.)

If the police chief is management-oriented, as he must be in a management-directed town such as Dallas, it follows that his men will be too. Speaking not of policemen but of the general citizenry, Dr. Harry Martin, sociologist at the University of Texas Medical School in Dallas, said, "After all, the significant reference group for white-collar workers is the boss. They will usually orient their behavior toward his."

When Oswald left the Texas Book Depository, he was stopped by a Dallas police officer. He was allowed to leave when the *manager* told the officer that Oswald worked there.

"Why in hell didn't he arrest the manager?" a visiting reporter asked in exasperation. "Even in detective stories on television, nobody leaves the room until he has been questioned. How did you know the manager didn't do it?"

But in Dallas the training is that management is benevolent and always does good. In calamitous situations, such as that which recently happened in Dallas, no police officer, despite his training, can be expected to react precisely and correctly to every development. In this case, the officer reacted as thousands of other

Dallas people would have reacted: the manager said Oswald was all right, so Oswald was all right. Later that afternoon, Oswald allegedly killed one officer and nearly killed another before he was caught.

Curry has taken full responsibility for the move of Oswald from the city to the county jail. He admits that this was timed according to the wishes of the press and television. Curry is a good, honest former truck driver who has progressed through the ranks of the police department to assistant chief and then to chief. No hint of graft or corruption has ever come anywhere near him, but you can't find anyone in Dallas who believes that Chief Curry made his fatal decision without some strong advice from somewhere. All men of influence in Dallas were anxious for the city to get the best possible press. Disaster had taken place despite their great effort to prevent it, and their thought was to try to come out of the whole horrifying mess with some shred of dignity left to the city.

"You have the nicest policemen to the press I have ever seen," Henri de Turenne of *France Soir* told me. "God help you!"

Actually, Sheriff Bill Decker had received an anonymous tip the night before that someone would try to shoot Oswald. He called Curry at 7:00 on that Sunday morning to try to get him to switch the time. Curry, manacled by his promises, stuck with them. In the same spirit, he and the chief investigating officer, Detective Captain Will Fritz, and District Attorney Henry Wade, had consistently answered reporters' questions throughout the hours. Whether in doing so they violated Oswald's civil rights would certainly have been a germane issue had Oswald come to trial.

Percy Foreman, the great Houston defense attorney, thinks Oswald could not have had a fair trial in Texas—or perhaps anywhere else—because of statements made before the man even was represented by a lawyer.

On the other hand, the press had its point, too. If Oswald had been acting for some special group, this fact could have set off rioting, group against group, all over America. It was important for the press to know and for the American people to know that he was a loner. This the police indicated quickly and the press published quickly.

In any case, the public relations policy of police cooperation with the press ended in the shooting of Lee Harvey Oswald by Jack Ruby, a man known personally to many police officers in Dallas.

In any downtown area of a metropolitan city there are people who resemble Jack Ruby. When I first met him I thought I'd known him before. I had, in a way: in Cincinnati, Kansas City, St. Louis, Minneapolis, Los Angeles and in New York. Their names were different, but these men were really one man, superficially; without attempting to prejudge Ruby's sanity, they may still be the same man. He deals in flesh—not in the real money-making use of flesh, but rather in the second-rate use of it, in burlesque or strip shows. He treats his girls like flesh; he may himself become involved with one of them, or sometimes all of them, but it is still a matter of flesh. He will give a girl a hundred dollars toward an operation, but this is impulsive emotionalism. He has no basic relationship with her and he will bawl her out for a lackluster performance, or for being late, as he would a total stranger.

If any kind of strong relationship between some woman and himself is going to come about, it will be with someone as far away from his strippers as he can get. (Ruby had two such relationships, both of which ended in failure.) He will fix a friend up with one of his girls, but what happens after that is up to the two of them. He promises nothing, takes no percentage. Towards his other employees, he is alternately generous and sentimental and sometimes almost psychopathically cruel; a hardship story will make him cry and bring out generosity, but forty-eight hours later he will have trouble remembering the girl's (or the man's) name. He could easily fire either one for a minor offense.

With visitors his conversation will be disjointed and

eventually emotional. Whatever the subject once was, it will change. He stutters and his eyes roam, as though seeking help. At one moment, the visitor will hear that the club is doing well, the next that the proprietor's mother is dying of cancer, and later that somebody ought to "pow that son of a bitch over in the corner" who is making so much noise. (This last is usually accompanied by the smacking of a fist into an open hand.)

Men like Ruby have come to whatever they are from the ghettos of the world. The symbol of authority has always been the cop on the beat, and this symbol persists. Those who reject it, fight it, and those who do not resist it, need it first as the mark of recognition and, second, as the mark of approval. The man who fights this authority is a gangster, the second is a Ruby; the one commits acts against society, the other has to know about them, to be on the inside, to know something the police do not know, to find out from the police what his friends do not know. Such special knowledge gives stature to such men, and satisfies the childhood yearning to be close to the man on the beat to identify with him.

The line between the policeman and the gangster is sometimes faint. Kids join the police force for many reasons, but one of them is a fascination with evil, or at least, with low life. Through the years, this fascination can progress until the cop identifies with the lower elements of human nature. In Dallas, as over all of America, many strippers have steadily dated members of the vice squad. Strippers are not to be equated with prostitutes, but they do not usually teach Bible class and they often double as B-girls. Experience in life has been similar for the girl and for the officer; after all, they keep the same hours.

Most good police officers are extremely proud of their underworld contacts. A good example is Sheriff Bill Decker of Dallas, who is generally considered one of the best police officers in the Southwest and possibly in the nation. Decker has been in the sheriff's office since 1933 and has been sheriff himself since 1948. Since then, nobody has even opposed him for this elective office for the simple reason that J. Edgar Hoover might well have trouble beating him in Dallas County. Decker knows so many crooks that when he cannot find one he simply leaves a message for the man to come in.

He couldn't find Dave Jarvis one day after Jarvis' bloody clothes were found near the body of one I. J. Poole, so he left his message. The next day, Jarvis appeared. "You want me, Bill?"

"Sure do, Dave," Decker said and charged him with murder.

One of the Southwest's most famous murderers, Raymond Hamilton, was trapped in the darkness of the Fort Worth railroad yards, and Decker went in after him. "Come on out, Raymond," Decker said.

"Is it Bill Decker?" Hamilton said.

"This is Bill."

With two guns on him, Hamilton came out without firing a shot—and went to the electric chair.

Decker could not possibly be as effective as he is without his underworld contacts and without their respect. He is scrupulously fair, and they know it. More than that, there is the strange psychological phenomenon of the attraction across that thin line of the hood toward the good cop. They understand each other. For instance, a thief may go on thieving; that's his living. But he will not lie to Bill Decker; that would be unthinkable.

So far as is known, Ruby never lived outside the law. He lived on its fringes, and the people around him lived on its fringes. He was a second-rater, and he knew it and hated it. For him recognition and approval were necessities—not just from people in general, but from people in authority. From his childhood, authority was the man on the beat. He would do almost anything for the liking and respect of a police officer.

"Give you his shirt," a young police officer told me. "I got so I quit going up there to his place. Never could pick up a check. I couldn't believe it when he shot Oswald. 'Not Jack Ruby!' I said. We all did. He's the best-hearted guy you ever saw."

The trial may or may not establish the reason Ruby killed Lee Oswald. The chances are it will not but will end, rather, in the same speculation we have had since it happened. The chances are that Ruby himself will not tell the truth simply because he doesn't know it. Looking at it coldly, one could say Ruby committed murder for three reasons: (1) after a lifetime of mediocrity he could be the most famous man in America (and in a way he is); (2) most people would approve of what he did (they do not, but at the time, a million Americans must have said aloud that they would like to kill Oswald); (3) he would probably get off with a light sentence (he may very well).

He could have killed Oswald for these reasons, and they probably did enter into his decision. But it was more complicated than that. This type of man, whether in Dallas or elsewhere, spends a lifetime seeking a status he can never have. His car is bigger than his apartment; people see his car and not his home. He carries more cash than he has in the bank; people notice the cash and do not examine his account. He will lend someone a hundred dollars when he does not know how he is going to pay his waitresses. He seeks identity in a world which refuses it. He looks for ways to rise in a world pushing down, and he finds all the wrong ways.

For some men, the weight of the American Dream is too heavy a burden.

7 | The news of the day

Outside of the Dallas police, who are in a class by themselves in this regard, no enterprise in the city has caught
the amount of abuse the *Dallas News* has taken since
the events of November. The paper lost several hundred
subscriptions, at least. Its owners and editors have been
pilloried in the American press, and especially in local

conversation. The paper has been blamed for creating a "climate of hate" in Dallas, and at least two men I know had the identical first reaction when hearing the news of the President's death: "Has anyone sent the *News* a telegram congratulating them?"

But this was when most people thought a right-winger had committed the murder. The immediate reaction against the paper was as emotional as everything else during those first hours and can be discounted. But a month after the assassination one of the most powerful men in Dallas, hearing of the *News'* difficulties, said simply, "Well, they had it coming."

There are two newspapers in Dallas, the *Morning News* and the evening *Times-Herald*. The *News* has traditionally had the greater circulation and influence of the two. The *Times-Herald* sells more copies in the city of Dallas, but the *News* is larger in the state and claims at the moment to have the highest circulation in Texas, i.e., nearly a quarter of a million. Until a few years ago, when the *Herald* began to reassess itself as a newspaper rather than as a handsome profit-making corporation, the *News* had a clear lead in terms of authority and leadership. This may be changing now. Many people are impressed with the quality of the *Herald*'s editorials since A. C. Greene, the literary editor, started writing them. These pieces have had point and have been remarkably tart for the *Herald*. But for many years the *Herald's* editorial page couldn't match the bite of the *News*.

Both papers are conservative, but the conservatism of the *News* over the past fifteen or twenty years has taken on the tone of the radical right. Its editorial page has been not just dissenting, but insulting. A dissenting newspaper is one thing; a frustrated and sneering newspaper is quite another. Since the end of the war, the *News* has seemed to stand for frustration rather than for enlightened dissent. All United States presidents since Franklin D. Roosevelt's day have been subject to its wrath—even Eisenhower, who was much too liberal in some of his policies for the *News*.

The late President Kennedy was once given a personal taste of the tone which the *News'* editorials have often taken. At a publishers' gathering in Washington, E. M. (Ted) Dealey, publisher of the *News*, informed the President that he represented the grass roots of Texas and said that these grass roots were in search of a man on a horse to lead them. But Kennedy, Dealey told him, was trying to lead the country "on Caroline's tricycle." This statement, made to the President of the United States, seemed to many people a bit extravagant and it gave the paper's critics ammunition in their charges that the *News* is irresponsible and reckless in matters of taste and discretion.

When Lyndon Johnson beat Coke Stevenson for the United States Senate, he won by eighty-seven votes and he did it by carrying a couple of south Texas counties, predominantly Mexican, whose voting strength was controlled by one man, George Parr. The *News*, which had backed Stevenson, immediately cried "Fraud!" and began a personal campaign against Johnson which reminded some people of Westbrook Pegler's vendetta against Eleanor Roosevelt. The tone was intense enough so that the reader could quite easily have got the impression that Johnson was no more than a common thief. The *News* did not make it clear to its readers that when Stevenson won the governorship of Texas he had carried the same Mexican counties by approximately the same margins, which would make it seem that Johnson simply outtalked his opponent for the Parr votes, quite a normal course of events in American politics.

During the several months before the assassination, the *News* moderated its approach to Johnson noticeably. Some *News* people and Johnson representatives had been anxious to arrange some kind of meeting at which editorial differences between the paper and the Vice President could be talked out at length. A weekend meeting was arranged at the LBJ ranch in Johnsonville. Besides Ted Dealey himself, other members of the *News* who went along included Joe Dealey, president of the paper; Jack B. Krueger, his managing editor; and Dick West, the chief editorial writer.

The ranch has great charm and provided the pleasantest atmosphere in which these men had met in a long time; and Johnson is, if possible, even more persuasive with his political opposition than he is with his friends. The meeting was frank and open, and it had a marked effect on the editorial policy of the paper. As things turned out, it may have saved the *News* embarrassment. By the time Johnson became President, the channels of communication were open, and the editorial page was able to wish him well with grace and sincerity.

Over the years, however, the *News'* editorials have been filled with anger. People of whom it disapproved it associated with Communism and subversion. The Supreme Court has been called a "judicial Kremlin." The New Deal was the "Queer Deal," and its policies were shaped by "an unknown number of subversives, perverts and miscellaneous security risks." The American Civil Liberties Union became the "Swivel" Liberties Union, and the *News* has taken a back seat to no one in its support of the witch-hunters.

Oddly enough, the *News* used to stand in precisely the opposite position. As Professor Paul F. Boller, Jr., pointed out in a searching analysis of the *News'* editorial position since the early 1930's the *Dallas News* was once a mildly New Deal, pro-Russian newspaper that favored U.S. recognition of the Russian government.

"During the late thirties," Boller writes, "the editors of the *News* defended freedom of the press for the daily worker, excoriated the drive of the Hearst press against academic freedoms, praised Roosevelt and Landon for coming out against teachers' loyalty oaths during the 1936 campaign, called Mayor Frank Hague 'un-American' and 'Hitleristic' for suppressing left-wing speakers in Jersey City and dismissed an inquiry by the Texas legislature into alleged Communism at the University of Texas as a needless investigation. Discussing 'Red-hunters in Texas' on October 17, 1936, the editors had this to say:

"'The trouble with many of the Red-hunters is that, while wholly honest, they are the gullible victims of racketeers who live luxuriously from the profits of Red scares. One of the easiest rackets to work in this country is to form a patriotic organization with high dues and expensive publications. The promoter then works up a few Red scares, and money from thousands of frightened suckers comes rolling in.'"

To the thousands of people who have been reading the *News* only since 1945, it will seem absolutely unbelievable that such words ever appeared in it. Most newspapers, as America learned more about Russian

Communism, veered from non-Communism to anti-Communism in the late forties. But if they had been enlightened, fair-minded newspapers before, they generally remained such. The *News* turned full circle. An editorial page which had once been a national model for thoughtfulness became a strident voice of opposition which seemed to encourage right-wing radicalism, acts of defiance, McCarthyism, super-patriotism and the rest.

As Professor Boller points out, this full circle is unpermissible, at least in one way. If recognition of Communist Russia was a "Queer Deal" plot, as it has insisted in recent years, then the *News* was a part of this plot, and a vocal, articulate part of it, and its readers should know this. In addition, it is one thing to change one's mind (and there must be few thinking people who have not changed theirs over these last twenty years), but it is another to change one's whole personality and character. This the *News* has succeeded in doing. It has not been the voice of dissent, but the voice of immoderate dissent, and that is what its critics mean when they charge the newspaper with being the single greatest umbrella for approval and encouragement of the radical right wing.

It is an easy charge to make; like most easy charges, it oversimplifies. The entire previous discussion has been concerned with one page of the newspaper. On its other pages, the *News* has maintained a superior product and has never to my knowledge imposed the views of its editorial page on its reporters or its columnists. In four years of working on the paper, I must have written close to two thousand stories for it; not one was ever cut out, cut down, rewritten or in any way changed to conform to editorial policy. I have heard many reporters say the same thing. I remember once when Dean Acheson came to town years ago and I was assigned to cover his visit. On the *News'* editorial page, no man in America was as much a whipping boy as was Acheson, then the United States Secretary of State. He had been accused of selling out China, fellow-traveling and everything else. But every word I wrote about Acheson's trip was printed as written and placed in the most prominent possible position on page one.

This same policy of fairness in the news columns has held true on scores of other controversial stories. In any political campaign, the *News* staff, under managing editor Krueger, will inevitably catch as much hell from the right as from the left, which usually means that a newspaper is balancing its coverage well. Columnists like John Rosenfield in amusements and Lon Tinkle in literature say what they wish to say within the bounds of their fields. The *News* is proud of its writers like Paul Crume, Frank X. Tolbert, Larry Grove, Bud Shrake and others, and it gives them loose rein in the expression of opinion. These days it is also publishing Walter Lippmann as a balance to its own views, though it has not always consistently printed the liberal views of others on its editorial page.

On November 22, 1963, the *News'* editorial welcoming Kennedy was in the spirit of the campaign for a friendly reception; it was gracious and charming. On the same day, however, the following advertisement was given a full page:

Welcome Mr. Kennedy
to Dallas . . .

. . . A city so disgraced by a recent liberal smear attempt that its citizens have just elected two more conservative Americans to public office.

. . . A city that is an economic "Boom Town," not because of Federal handouts, but through conservative economic and business practices.

. . . A city that will continue to grow and prosper despite efforts by you and your administration to penalize it for its non-conformity to "new frontierism."

. . . A city that rejected your philosophy and policies in 1960 and will do so again in 1964—even more emphatically than before.

Mr. Kennedy, despite contentions on the part of your administration, the State Department, the Mayor of Dallas, the Dallas City Council and members of your party, we free-thinking and American-thinking citizens of Dallas still have, through a constitution largely ignored by you, the right to address our grievances, to question you, to disagree with you, and to criticize you.

In asserting this constitutional right, we wish to ask you publicly the following questions—indeed, questions of paramount importance and interest to all free peoples everywhere—which we trust you will answer . . . in public, without sophistry.

These questions are:

Why is Latin America turning either anti-American or Communistic or both, despite increased U.S. foreign aid, State Department policy, and your own ivory tower pronouncements?

Why do you say we have built a "wall of freedom" around Cuba when there is no freedom in Cuba today? Because of your policy, thousands of Cubans have been imprisoned, are starving and being persecuted—with thousands already murdered and thousands more awaiting execution and, in addition, the entire population of almost 7,000,000 Cubans are living in slavery.

Why have you approved the sale of wheat and corn to our enemies when you know the communist soldiers "travel on their stomachs" just as ours do? Communist soldiers are daily wounding and/or killing American soldiers in South Viet Nam.

Why did you host, salute and entertain Tito— Moscow's Trojan horse—just a short time after our sworn enemy, Khrushchev, embraced the Yugoslav dictator as a great hero and leader of communism?

Why have you urged greater aid, comfort, recognition, and understanding for Yugoslavia, Poland, Hungary, and other communist countries while turning your back on the pleas of Hungarian, East German, Cuban and other anti-communist freedom fighters?

Why did Cambodia kick the U. S. out of its country after we poured nearly 400 million dollars of aid into its ultra-leftist government?

Why has Gus Hall, head of the U. S. Communist Party, praised almost every one of your policies and announced that the party will endorse and support your re-election in 1964?

Why have you banned the showing at U. S. military bases of the film "Operation Abolition"—the movie by the House Committee on Un-American Activities exposing communism in America?

Why have you ordered or permitted your brother Bobby, the Attorney General, to go soft on communists, fellow-travelers, and ultra-leftists in America, while permitting him to persecute loyal Americans who criticize you, your administration, and your leadership?

Why are you in favor of the U. S. continuing to give economic aid to Argentina, in spite of the fact that Argentina has just seized almost 400 million dollars of American private property?

Why has the foreign policy of the United States degenerated to the point that the C. I. A. is arranging coups and having staunch anti-communist allies of the U. S. bloodily exterminated?

Why have you scrapped the Monroe Doctrine in favor of the Spirit of Moscow?

Mr. Kennedy, as citizens of these United States of America, we demand answers to these questions, and we want them now.

The American Fact Finding Committee

An unaffiliated and non-partisan group of citizens who wish truth

Bernard Weissman,

Chairman

P. O. Box 1792—Dallas 21, Texas

The advertisement was what might be called semi-inflammatory. It was certainly no worse than others which have been printed by the *News* and other newspapers over the years. But in the explosive atmosphere of Dallas at the time and in the wake of monumental efforts to keep the people calm, this advertisement infuriated a large section of the community.

When the advertisement leapt to the national attention, the American Jewish Committee immediately investigated Weissman and found that he is a carpet salesman who had been in Dallas a couple of weeks. The committee also found that the money to pay for the ad was raised among the usual crowd of Dallas right-wingers. It theorized that a Jewish name was attached to it to escape the frequent charges of anti-Semitism which are leveled against these groups. It was, in the kindest possible terms, a shoddy thing to appear in the paper on that morning, and it dismayed many of the *News'* own staffmen even more than it did the general public. Newspapers are not models of efficiency, and ads of this kind sometimes sneak into print by accident because no one has stopped them. Nevertheless the ad did appear, and the *News* has had to live with that fact ever since.

The *News* calls itself the oldest business institution in Texas, and in its long history it has had some proud moments. It is principally responsible for running the Ku Klux Klan out of Texas. The paper's stand cost it immeasurably in terms of circulation and advertising revenues. But it fought the Klan and won; the organization has never had any power or influence in Texas because the *News*, under Ted Dealey's father, G. B. Dealey, made the Ku Klux Klan a group to scorn rather than to respect. Joe Dealey, the young president of the paper, is this remarkable man's grandson. Out of the sorrows of these days in Dallas may come his chance, aided by the able and reflective men around him, to lead the city thoughtfully and purposefully to better things; and the oldest business institution in Texas may rise to other proud moments as our years continue.

8 | The fate of the arts

The super-patriotic thinking of the far right in Dallas
got some national attention back in 1955 and 1956 in
controversies involving the Dallas Public Library and
the Dallas Museum of Fine Arts. Actually, as it turned
out, the library wasn't involved for very long. It opened
an exhibition in 1956 of works by modern artists. One
of the artists was Pablo Picasso, who has often stated

that he is a communist, though it isn't likely that the Kremlin counts on him as a leader of the world-wide conspiracy.

The telephones started ringing barely minutes after the exhibition had opened. After a short consultation with one of the city councilmen, the library director, James Meeks, ordered the Picasso painting and rug taken down to eliminate controversy. This provoked John Rosenfield, writing in the *Dallas News* a few days later, to suggest a credo for the city concerning the exhibition of paintings, the performance of music, the circulation of books and so on. The credo, he said, should be, "If anybody objects, yank it down or ban it from the halls or burn it up." He suggested that one day the citizens of Dallas might be in the unusual position of looking at a brassiered Venus de Milo.

Before it was over, the art museum controversy, which dragged on for more than a year, came before the Dallas City Council, nearly got one American Legion man sued for libel by *Time* and *Life*, brought down a rain of national editorials, and finally involved the United States Government.

The Museum of Fine Arts in Dallas is partially supported by city tax money. The city puts up about $66,000 every year for its maintenance and staffing, but no tax money is used for acquisitions. When the museum wishes to buy something, it uses money it has raised from donors, charity balls and other campaigns. Nevertheless, since the staff and the building are publicly supported, the citizenry at large has a stake in it. Up until 1955, there had been some minor skirmishing on what work should be hung and what should not be hung in the museum. Then the board of directors of the museum issued a statement saying, "It is not our policy knowingly to acquire or to exhibit the work of a person known by us to be now a Communist or of Communist-front affiliation." As a result paintings by Picasso, Diego Rivera and others were removed from the museum walls.

The attack on the pictures (or, rather, on the artists) had come from patriotic groups such as the Public Affairs Luncheon Club, the Inwood Lions Club, a post of the American Legion and others. The museum trustees' rather weak position was immediately attacked in *Art News* in an editorial the essence of which stated, "The conclusions of civilized man over these problems are that we judge the work of art and not its author unless he intrudes himself or his ideas extraneous to art upon that work. It has taken much wisdom and a good deal of blood over many generations of western man to learn that lesson and to make it into a civilized tradition."

Not long after this, the trustees again found themselves under fire in Dallas because of certain works included in the historic "Family of Man," a photo-graphic exhibition put together by Edward Steichen. What worried the trustees was that a few of the five hundred-odd pictures carried credit lines of Soviet photographers. One of them even had a Russian prov-erb as a caption: "Eat bread and salt and speak the truth." (There was also an issue over an expressive pic-ture of childbirth and a poetical one of lovers, although the Museum of Fine Arts stands not five hundred yards from the Health Museum, where anatomical reproduc-tive processes are always on exhibition.) Steichen him-self, getting wind of the controversy over the two photographs, telephoned the Dallas Museum to say that his exhibition must be shown as an entity or not at all. "It wouldn't surprise me if this were going on in Vermont or New Hampshire," he said. "Up in New England they think that babies come out of cabbages; but in Texas . . ." Finally, "The Family of Man" was displayed as originally planned and was one of the record attractions of the Dallas Museum of Fine Arts.

The board of trustees, having been castigated by *Art News*, reflected on its earlier policy and in December, 1955, changed it. The new policy read that the Dallas Museum of Fine Arts "is to exhibit and acquire works of art only on the basis of their merit as works of art, exercising the best judgment to preserve the integrity of the Museum of Art as a municipal institution." The

Dallas News inadvertently dealt the trustees a blow by headlining its story: MUSEUM SAYS REDS CAN STAY. This brought on a predictable letter from Colonel John W. Mayo, Chairman of the Communism-in-Arts Committee of the Dallas County Patriotic Council. Colonel Mayo explained that his council represented sixteen Dallas patriotic and civic associations. The organizations represented were the Southern Memorial Association, the D.A.R., the Daughters of 1812, the Matheon Club, the Inwood Lions Club, the Bassett Art Club, the Oak Cliff Art Association, the Federation of Dallas Artists, the Klepper Club, the Reaugh Art Club, the Veterans of Foreign Wars, the American Legion (Metropolitan Post), the Public Affairs Luncheon Club, the Pro-America and the 1950 Study Club.

Colonel Mayo's letter of protest did not just object to the trustees' new policy; it also objected to a show the museum had scheduled. The show was called "Sports in Art," and it was co-sponsored in Dallas by *Sports Illustrated*, one of the Luce magazines, and by Neiman-Marcus. George Trescher of the magazine and I had worked out the details in New York some months before. The indignation and the name-calling which the show aroused bewildered both of us; it may have been politically the most inoffensive art show ever put together. The Patriotic Council was aiming its fire at the work of four artists: Ben Shahn, Leon Kroll, Yasuo

Kuniyoshi and William Zorach. The Council objected that these men had Communist or Communist-front records. The show was distributed by the American Federation of Arts and it had already been seen at the Boston Museum of Fine Arts and the Corcoran Gallery in Washington. No protests or attempts at censorship occurred in either city. The show was also scheduled to be sent to the Australian Olympics in November by the United States Information Agency. The pictures involved were "Skaters" by Kuniyoshi, "The Park" and "Winter" by Leon Kroll, "Fisherman" by William Zorach and "National Pastime" by Ben Shahn. Skating, fishing, baseball and looking at a park are generally considered non-subversive activities, but the Patriotic Council argued that though none of these men had ever been called a Communist, they had lent their names to some organizations that the House Un-American Activities Committee had called Communist fronts.

The trustees refused to change their new policy and the Patriotic Council went before the Dallas Park Board which actually controls the museum's city funds. But before doing so, the council had its own meeting in the Highland Park Town Hall auditorium, which was packed, and the leaders of the Patriotic Council explained their thinking.

"The highest courts in the land," said Colonel Alvin M. Owsley, principal speaker, "have upheld the acts

of Congress in declaring the Red Communist organization is not a political party but a 'criminal conspiracy
to destroy the republic by means of force and violence.' "
Mrs. Florence Rogers, who was president of the Patriotic Council at the time, quoted from some recent news
stories on Communist cold-war policy and stated that
she would like to think "our Dallas is a citadel of safety
against these insidious threats." Colonel Mayo stated
that he did not wish any of his tax money in the pockets
of Communist artists, but Mr. William Ware, a vice
president of the council and also a vice commander of
the American Legion Metropolitan Post, really stirred
up the meeting when he said, "Certainly no one has
ever called *Time* magazine an anti-Communist publication." When he had recovered his wits, Frank Mc-
Culloch, *Time-Life* bureau chief in Dallas, warned Mr.
Ware that any further statements along these lines
would be presented to *Time-Life* attorneys.

Meanwhile the newspapers were deluged with letters, most of them on the side of the censors. The *Times-
Herald* wrote an editorial of approximately 250 words
in which it said virtually nothing, and the *News* wrote
one in which, after apparently siding with the trustees,
it stated that the trustees were sometimes quite wrong
and the final judgment should be made by the public.
"Even art exhibitions stand up by that opinion, whether
it is shared or not by the sophisticated and the dilet-

tante" said the *News*. Most of the liberal trustees would much rather have had the *News'* opposition than this backhanded support.

When the Patriotic Council finally went before the Park Board, William Ware again stole the show by citing the Dallas Art Museum's "long record" of displaying the work of Communist artists or of fellow-travelers. Before he was through he managed to give the impression that the museum itself looked to him like a Communist-front organization, a staggering concept when one reviews the capitalistic wealth in the hands of its trustees. In spite of all of this furor, which was stirring up art columns in many other cities, the Park Board backed its museum's board of trustees, and the pictures went up as scheduled. Nobody picketed the opening as had been threatened, but they did distribute Patriotic Council literature. The Patriotic Council didn't give up. Eventually it went to the City Council itself, but the latter defended its Park Board and, by implication, its museum trustees.

The sad part of all of this was that the exhibition never did get to the Olympics in Australia. In Dallas the men who could see no subversion in a baseball picture by Ben Shahn won the day. In Washington, the USIA withdrew the exhibition from the Olympics. According to the *New York Times*, the USIA stated that some of the artists did not pass its political tests and the *Times* indicated that the USIA was afraid of the reactions of a few Congressmen. "The USIA," said the *Times*, "is implying that art must undergo a test of the political legitimacy of the artist . . . uncomfortably close to the Nazi and Communist concept. . . ."

In Dallas there was noise, but censorship lost; in Washington, no noise, but censorship won.

Museums are not the only targets of those who would impose censorship for "patriotic" or "moral" reasons. As a free-thinking people, we have to deal also with the censorship of books and ideas. As one would expect, Texas has not gone through this battle unscarred.

When Henry Miller's *Tropic of Cancer* arrived in Dallas, the outcry was such that the police paid a visit to all the bookstores and "persuaded" their managers to take the book off sale. It has not since reappeared. Yet this is a book considered by many people of judgment to be a work of art. Others, including myself, feel that Miller, having a serious purpose, missed his goal and produced an unsuccessful book. Nevertheless, *Tropic of Cancer* has been the object of much literary controversy for more than a quarter century and the concept that a police officer should be in a position to be able to tell people what to read and what not to read is unthinkable.

Dallas, of course, was not the only city in which

Tropic of Cancer had its troubles. At one time in 1962 it was unavailable in more than half of the country. But in the other half of the country it was and is available, and a number of courts have found that the book is not obscene as defined by law. Obscene in some cities and not in others, *Tropic of Cancer* became a problem for the retail bookseller. The publisher, Grove Press, said that it would defend booksellers who were arrested, but most of the reputable booksellers, in Dallas at least, felt that the book wasn't worth the time and trouble. It is also quite possible that they were not anxious to encourage an attack on their ranks by such organizations as the White Citizens' Council, the National Indignation Committee, the John Birch Society, the Friends of General Walker and Texans for America. The people who lead attacks on the morality of certain books often do so on patriotic grounds. The books they label immoral are, the reasoning goes, part of a Communist conspiracy. It seems that such books will pervert the morals of our youth and destroy the country from within.

A famous case was the attack in Houston against a book which contained a biography of Plato. It was led by Mrs. Fay Seale, who said that she was a member of the John Birch Society. She was irritated with Plato because he talked about "communal living and free love and such." She went on to say that Plato's ideas probably contributed to the number of sex maniacs walking the streets. This provoked the *Milwaukee Journal* to comment: "The suggestion that school children are rushing to read Plato or read about him is startling. Educators everywhere ought to find out how Houston does it."

In Midland, Texas, a number of books were removed from the library shelves because it was alleged that some four-letter words appeared in them. They were books of established reputation: *Andersonville* by MacKinlay Kantor. *The Grapes of Wrath* by John Steinbeck, *Laughing Boy* by Oliver La Farge, *Of Time and the River* by Thomas Wolfe, *The Big Sky* and *The Way West* by A. B. Guthrie, Jr., *Marjorie Morningstar* by Herman Wouk, *1984* by George Orwell, *Brave New World* by Aldous Huxley and *The Portable Steinbeck*. They were attacked partly as a device of the Communist conspiracy to lower the morals of youth.

John Howard Griffin is a Texas writer who ran into some of these same problems himself with his first novel, *The Devil Rides Outside*. Since then he has written another book, *Black Like Me*, an extraordinary account of his journey through the South disguised as a Negro. This second book had a predictable effect among the people of Mansfield, Texas (just outside Fort Worth), where Griffin lives. He has been hanged in effigy and has suffered other indignities since the book's publication. Writing of the censorship problem, he has said in the *Southwest Review:*

"Every obscenity law must stipulate that the book be considered *as a whole.* A book cannot legally be held as an obscene libel merely because it *contains* certain words or phrases. At one time smut-hunters banned most of the world's literature by going through books and making lists of all 'offensive words and phrases.' Laws that permitted this piecemeal evaluation of a work were called 'containing statute legislation.' This was declared unconstitutional in the United States Supreme Court decision in *Butler v. Michigan.* Censorship activities in Texas have invariably returned to the practice of excerpting words or phrases with the view of denouncing the work because it *contains them.* Works *containing* ideas that offend group prejudices are also banned on this basis. We have witnessed again and again the spectacle of people 'opposing' books even in court, without having read them. A list of words or ideas was enough to convince them. The Texas House Committee, investigating textbooks, decided after weeks of testimony that they would accept no further statements until the witness had actually read the books he condemned."

The investigating committee of state-used textbooks

was called together after complaints from various far right organizations about "patriotic aspects" of the books. In this case, the leading organization was Texans for America and its spokesman was J. Evetts Haley. These people objected to mentions of the United Nations, Franklin D. Roosevelt and to the very word 'communism.' Mr. Haley's thesis was that "the stressing of both sides of the controversy only confuses the young and encourages them to make snap judgments based on insufficient evidence. Until they are old enough to understand both sides of the question, they should be taught only the American side." All this means is that the textbooks would become a form of brainwashing. Fact would be ignored or distorted to fit concepts. Whatever mistakes this country has made would be eliminated from written history. Indeed, history itself would be eliminated and the students would be reduced to building their minds by reading long fictions —and pretty dull ones at that, since most of the good writers, it will be remembered, have already been eliminated due to their use of bad words.

Fortunately, some writers like J. Frank Dobie, Lon Tinkle, literary editor of the *Dallas News*, Frank Wardlaw of the University of Texas Press, and others, finally got aroused enough to make the journey to Austin and issue indignant protests. The efforts to rewrite the textbooks failed, at least for the time being. They did not fail, however, before the citizenry had been offered a suggested technique of brainwashing that is no more defensible than the system of the Communists themselves.

9 | November 1960: The visit of Lyndon B. Johnson

The ability of the human brain to remember only what it wants to remember, and of the human eye to see only what it wants to see, is seldom better documented than it is in the case of a visit that Senator Lyndon B. Johnson and his wife made to Dallas shortly before the election in 1960. A reporter can find as many versions of what happened as he can find people who were there and it seems at this point that nearly everyone was there. About the only thing on which everyone agrees is where it happened.

The corner of Commerce and Akard Streets in downtown Dallas has been for years the site of football rallies, mass prayer meetings and other public demonstrations. On one side of Commerce stands the Baker Hotel; on the side stands the Adolphus. Until a few years ago they were the two major hotels in town and though now there are others, this location remains the most popular rally site in the city.

For instance, when the University of Texas and Oklahoma University come to town for their annual football game in the Cotton Bowl, the hotels remove all furniture from the lobbies and hire all the extra house detectives they can get. The party is held on all floors of both hotels, in the street and sometimes on the roofs. The celebrations go on into the night, whiskey and beer flow openly in the streets and no citizen of Dallas would consider going downtown on the eve of the game. In spite of efforts by the police to be as understanding as possible, it was necessary last year to make 136 arrests during the course of the good-natured evening. For mob scenes, then, Commerce and Akard is *the* place in Dallas.

Friday, November 4, 1960, had been designated for months as Republican "Tag Day" in Dallas. This is an innocent occasion on which about three hundred good-looking girls roam the downtown streets in two shifts, one aimed at people going to work, the other at those headed towards lunch. On the Friday in question, the girls, a lot of whom were Junior Leaguers, wore a little red coif hat, a white blouse, a red vest with a gold watch chain to which many had attached a large Nixon button, and a dark blue skirt. "Nixon" was written across the back of the vest. Each volunteeer carried a big model's handbag with a Nixon-Lodge sign on it, filled with tags and folders.

Long after Republican Tag Day had been announced, it was discovered that Senator Johnson's last stop in Dallas would coincide with it. This was purely coincidental. The Democrats scheduled a luncheon for Johnson at the Adolphus Hotel.

On the actual day the Republicans had added some signs for the occasion. In addition to the Nixon-Lodge signs, which they had planned to carry, many of the girls carried signs saying, "Lyndon Go Home." The intersection of Commerce and Akard was packed with people and so were the lobbies of both the Baker and the Adolphus Hotels.

The Johnsons arrived with Congressman Jim Wright (Democrat, of Fort Worth) and Mrs. Elizabeth Forsling Harris, then attached to the Senator's staff during the campaign. They made their way into the Baker lobby to wash and rest up in a suite which the Johnsons traditionally took during their stays in Dallas. By this time, the girls assigned to do the tagging had a lot of unsolicited help from the riff-raff from the beer parlors and some of the lower class restaurants in and around the area who had joined their ranks. As Mrs. Harris tells it, "There were a lot of low-type people mixed up with all those Junior Leaguers by the time Mr. Johnson reached the lobby. There was booing and hissing and Mrs. Johnson turned white. The Senator put her in the elevator and strolled back into the lobby himself. 'You ought to be glad you live in a country where you have the legal right to boo and hiss at a man who is running for the Vice Presidency of the United States,' he said to the crowd.

"For a moment, there was silence and I thought maybe he'd calmed them down but then out of the back, from one of these cheap guys who had left his beer long enough to join us, came this loud voice: 'Louder and funnier, Lyndon.'

"When we got upstairs, Senator Johnson was furious and Mrs. Johnson was obviously shaken. The street intersection was still a madhouse of people. Some of the hosts for the luncheon at which the Senator was to speak came up to the suite to suggest that the Johnsons go out a side door and enter the Adolphus by a side door in order to avoid the crowds. They also suggested that they could give the Senator a bull horn so that he could speak to the crowd if it should get unruly.

"The Senator told them he wanted nothing. He said, 'No, I only hope the day never comes when a man cannot walk his lady across the street in Dallas. I don't want anything more than the right to walk my wife across the street to lunch.'"

Mrs. Harris and Congressman Jim Wright preceded Senator and Mrs. Johnson to the Adolphus. Near the lobby entrance they met Congressman Bruce Alger, Republican of Dallas. Mrs. Harris gives this version of their exchange: "Jim Wright spoke to Alger and said that while he and Alger had had many disagreements, he still didn't think it appropriate for United States Congressmen to be standing in the middle of this mob scene holding an anti-Johnson placard. He pointed out that Johnson was the Senate Majority Leader and due even more respect than that from someone in Congress. Alger replied that he and his supporters were going to show Johnson that he was not wanted in Dallas. Everything Alger said was approved and applauded by the crowd behind him. In what he was saying, he seemed to gain encouragement from the crowd and his statements grew more extravagant. Congressman Wright finally gave up and walked away."

One thing no one disputes about what happened in the next few minutes: Senator Lyndon Johnson, Majority Leader of the Senate, and his wife were the center of a mob scene both in the streets of Dallas and in the lobby of the Adolphus Hotel. Mrs. Johnson was white, frightened and close to tears. At one point, in the middle of the street, she began to say something to the assembled crowd, but her husband gently put his finger on her lips. She could never have been heard, anyway, in the pandemonium.

Mr. Johnson described it from Houston on television the following night: "We were hissed at and spat upon, and two women were hurt in a mob scene that looked like some other country. It was hard to believe that this was happening in Dallas and in Texas."

John G. Tower, the Texas Republican Senatorial candidate at the time, had been in the Adolphus lobby. He issued a statement to the press the next day. "The Nixon supporters were almost all Dallas housewives while the Johnson partisans were nearly all men. It should be made clear that the Nixon ladies were spirited but orderly. It was the Johnson people, led by some huge men, who got mad and started all the pushing and shoving.

"Let's get the record straight. Senator Johnson exaggerated this demonstration out of all proportion to what actually happened. Both Senator and Mrs. Johnson were impeccably groomed when they entered the ballroom of the Adolphus Hotel following their reception."

A day or two after the initial story a *Dallas News* reporter said that she was also in the lobby of the hotel and did not see any indignity, although she admitted that the hundreds of chanting, pressing people were a mob. She also said Mrs. Johnson's coiffure was mussed.

But Maurice Levy, an NBC-TV cameraman who covered the occasion, said, "They certainly spat on them, although I don't know whether any of it landed. It was a mess."

Still another girl who was there, a young Junior Leaguer and a supporter of Alger, said, "It was certainly a mob scene. There's no question about that. I had my own clothes ripped, but it was not a 'hate' mob scene or a violent mob scene; it was too many people pressed too close—like a football game scene. I certainly never saw anybody spit at the Johnsons."

Yet another woman who was present says that she herself was fearful. "People were calling names and using phrases I had never heard at any kind of political gatherings. Don't let anybody tell you there wasn't hostility in that mob, because there was. I'm not saying it came from the 'tag girls' and it certainly didn't originate from them. It originated from the bums and a few of the 'tag girls' got caught up in the spirit. You know what mobs are like."

At the luncheon itself, Attorney General Will Wilson of Texas, who introduced Senator Johnson, said the demonstration outside did not reflect the "true spirit of Dallas." Johnson himself said that it made him sad that "we have people—attractive people, nice people—who can be so frustrated and so discourteous and so desperate."

Later on, Congressman Alger was quoted by a reporter as saying that the demonstration given Johnson was a "hubbub of a large gathering fighting for a society free from federal control." He added that "those who claim that there was jostling and jeering are thinking about the lobby of the hotel, and I was not there."

In the end it was none of the comments that lingered in the mind. It was a picture of Congressman Bruce Alger on the front page of the *Dallas Times-Herald* carrying an anti-Johnson placard, and it was the television coverage given by Levy and his colleagues which told the story in pictures without comment. Finally, it was Senator Johnson's comment in Houston the following day, combined with these picture stories, that aroused the press of the state and of the country to denounce the city as inhospitable and discourteous. Quite typical was a *Wichita Falls Times* editorial which said in part, "The organized mob demonstration which produced a highly volatile and out-of-hand situation that developed in downtown Dallas Friday is an event which blights the 1960 campaign scene not only for Texas but for the nation and the entire world."

Whatever the Republicans did or did not do on that Friday, they lost Texas the following Tuesday. There were many serious observers in Texas who will tell you that Nixon lost Texas by a shadow instead of winning it by a shadow largely because Congressman Bruce Alger was carrying a placard in front of the Adolphus Hotel.

10 | UN Day: The visit
of Adlai E. Stevenson

The third event that brought Dallas national and international attention in terms of its far right movement was the incident involving Adlai Stevenson. Mr. Stevenson, the United States Ambassador to the United Nations, came to Dallas on October 24, 1963, to address a United Nations Day meeting in Dallas. Stevenson had twice been the Democratic candidate for his country's highest office.

Just before United Nations Day, an extremist right-wing organization called the National Indignation Committee, headed by one Frank McGeehee, set aside a day and called it United States Day. A United States Day ceremony was scheduled in the Dallas Memorial Auditorium Theater, which seats about 2,000, for exactly twenty-four hours before United Nations Day.

About 1,200 people attended the ceremony, and roughly double that number attended the ceremonies on United Nations Day. United States Day caused no incident, while United Nations Day did. Before it was over, Adlai Stevenson had been spat upon and struck over the head with a placard, and Dallas was front-page news across America and throughout the world.

"We booked Memorial Theater for the Stevenson meeting," Jack Goren, chairman of the United Nations Day Committee, said, "because we were hopeful that one of the Dallas TV stations would televise the occasion. KRLD-TV [CBS] responded and agreed to televise the program.

"We had a press conference some two and a half to three weeks before UN Day. We announced in the newspaper what we were proposing to do. From my conversations with the people at Memorial Theater, General Walker [Major General Edwin Walker], upon hearing of our meeting (about one week prior to this), booked the same auditorium the night before for U. S. Day.

"About a week prior to the UN Day celebration we became concerned that there might be picketing at Memorial Theater. This concern was brought about by the fact that some young students who were out at the state fair were entertained at the home of a local person and one or two of them reported to their parents that they observed some pickets derogatory to the United Nations at the home of General Walker. Whether this was actually true or not we were never sure, and we have no proof of it. However, we did observe that there were cars with signs on the Dallas streets reading U. S. DAY OR UNITED NATIONS DAY—THERE MUST BE A CHOICE; YOU CANNOT RIDE BOTH HORSES, or words to that effect. This was the propaganda circulating on the Dallas streets, apparently put out by General Walker's supporters. General Walker was billed as the feature speaker for U. S. Day the night before UN Day.

"As you probably know, U. S. Day was designated two or three years ago by ultra-right wing groups in the United States but primarily in a few selected areas such as Arizona, Texas and California. Out of the 365 days of the year, they picked the day before the UN Day celebration, which has been in effect since 1948. The reason for the selection of that date is obvious, but so far as we were able to determine, U. S. Day has not gotten off the ground anywhere but the three areas that I mentioned; and mostly in few parts of Texas and Arizona."

At this point, the supporters of the United Nations Day suffered a real shock when Governor John Connally of Texas issued an official proclamation of United States Day in Texas (UN Day had been proclaimed long before). This provoked some immediate correspondence between Jack Goren and Governor Connally's office. Goren expressed his dismay that the governor had apparently given respectability to an occasion which was drummed up purely for the purpose of discrediting UN Day and the United Nations itself. He questioned whether the governor had known before issuing the proclamation that Major General Walker, a clear-cut representative of the far right wing, was to be the principal speaker.

The governor replied that he had not, as Goren suspected, been aware before the proclamation's issuance that Walker would be the chief speaker on UN Day, that in fact some kind of observance had been in effect before his time, and that he had been requested by a number of people to issue a proclamation for the occasion. He gave Goren the definite impression that he was not in any way trying to encourage General Walker and his supporters.

"It was a nice letter from the governor," Goren said, "and it made me feel a good deal better. The major thing worrying me was not that something called United States Day should be proclaimed as an official observance. The curse of this town has been that these things get into the hands of extremists. Then, one way or another, through the newspapers, public statements or whatever, the actions of the extremists get to seem all right, defensible, respectable. Nobody blasts them and tells them that their actions are impossible in civilized communities. I think that's the basic difference between Dallas and other places. Anyway, I venture that there will be no further proclamations of U. S. Day so long as it is in the control of the extremist elements which run it now."

During this time before the ambassador's visit, the premonition of some kind of trouble began to build. This was based in part simply on what kind of man Stevenson is and the feelings he inspires. This man—intellectual, internationalist, brilliant speaker—seems capable of arousing an emotion in Americans that is almost unique. His supporters are militant, as evidenced by the Democratic National Convention of 1960; his detractors are no less so. He is not a man who provokes a mild reaction.

Goren's task was to do everything he could to prevent the premonition of trouble from turning into reality. "I asked a security representative, Mr. William de Gan (a former agent for the Federal Bureau of Investigation, now employed in Dallas), who knows police chief Jesse Curry, to go down to the police department and to tell them of our concern about picketing. I was anxious to make sure that we would have adequate police protection at the theater because of what we had already learned. Also, we were sure General Walker would stir up his meeting in opposition to United Nations Day and to Mr. Stevenson.

"Mr. de Gan went there personally and spoke to Jesse Curry and was assured that there would be adequate police protection.

"A few days later reports began to come back to us that the picketing might be extreme and de Gan again went down to the police station and made arrangements for more extensive protection. The extra police were supposed to arrive at approximately 7:30 P.M.

"U. S. Day drew approximately 1,200 people. We monitored the meeting. This made us extremely aware that there would be large-scale attempts to picket and possibly do other things at our meeting the next night. We realized this from the tone of General Walker's speech, which aroused his audience to a high pitch about United Nations Day, that it was a part of the world-wide communist movement, the usual stuff with which you are familiar.

"We were, of course, concerned, but we had confidence that the police protection would be adequate.

"When I arrived at about 7:30 P.M., I found that the theater had already been infiltrated with numerous supporters of U. S. Day—complete with their flags, complete with their signs, complete with their noise-makers, which we were, of course, not aware that they would even attempt to use. The pickets did not show up in force until approximately 7:45. The police protection at the early stages was inadequate and in my judgment was never adequate or timely.

"If I had to say what the really terrible thing was, I would say that as bad as the picketing was, as bad as the mob action that took place as a part of the picketing was, and as bad as the spitting and hitting incident was —even worse was the hooting, the yelling, the noise makers, the waving of the flags, the waving of the signs, the attempt to break up the meeting itself by the followers of General Walker, the John Birch groups, and by the supporters of Mr. Frank McGeehee of the National Indignation Committee. This to me was totally undemocratic and un-American. The attempt to deny the American Ambassador to the United Nations the opportunity to express his ideas and the ideas of the United States government on world peace—this to me was the terrible, sad thing.

"Fortunately, it all was photographed. It was all heard by several hundred thousand people on live television. Coupled with the terrible incident that took place afterward, the Dallas community was faced with the fact that the extreme right wing had gone too far.

"After the meeting, we had a reception in the Memorial Theater on the stage for UN People. There was no attempt made to infiltrate that, but the pickets remained outside in numbers of seventy-five to 150 and they were organized in a group. About forty-five minutes after the meeting was over, roughly 9:45, we left with police escort to try to go to the cars. Apparently there was a woman screaming at Mr. Stevenson. He walked into the crowd, leaving the line of the police escort, merely to ask her what she was screaming at him about and to try to quiet her down. This resulted in the hitting incident by the woman and the spitting incident by the young student. When Mr. Stevenson was rescued by the police, he was brought to the limousine. He was in a state of shock, so to speak. He just could not understand that in America this sort of thing would happen, certainly not to him or to anyone. He has been used to picketing, but never to violence of this kind against representatives of the American government by Americans. He could not understand this. While he was wiping off the saliva with his handkerchief, his only comment was, 'Are these human beings or are these animals?' "

The woman who struck Mr. Stevenson was the wife of an insurance man who is prominent in one of the downtown luncheon clubs, and who was not even present at the United Nations Day meeting. When it was all over, her husband told a friend that he had not been able to make an outgoing phone call from his home or office for two or three days after the incident. The line was jammed with calls from people protesting his wife's action. She claimed that someone had pushed her, but the television film indicates no such thing.

The man who spat on Stevenson was a college student, Robert Edward Hatfield of Irving. Mr. Stevenson did not prefer charges against either person, but Hatfield made the mistake of also spitting on patrolman L. R. Larsen. According to Chief Assistant District Attorney A. D. (Jim) Bowie, it is a much more serious offense to spit on a policeman than it is to spit on the Ambassador to the United Nations. If one man commits assault on another, Texas law regards it as simple assault under most circumstances. The penalty would be a fine but no jail term. For aggravated assault against a police officer, however, the constitution prescribes a two-year jail term and a $1,000 fine, which is the maximum sentence.

Mr. Stevenson himself, though stunned by the violence of the evening, was in complete command of the heckling. When the police finally escorted Frank Mc-Geehee to a side door, Mr. Stevenson said, "For my part, I believe in the forgiveness of sin and the redemption of ignorance."

On October 28 the Dallas City Council, shocked and embarrassed by what had happened, unanimously adopted an anti-harassment ordinance to protect visiting speakers. It prohibits any person or groups from "interfering with a public or private assembly by the use of insulting, threatening or obscene language or intimidation."

The City Council and Mayor Cabell apologized to Stevenson on behalf of their city but Congressman Bruce Alger stated that the city had no reason at all to feel disgraced. Hatfield, he said, in one of his reports to his constituents, "lost his head because of his resentment against the UN that threatens his freedom and his country's freedom."

Alger did not state that he approved of hitting people and spitting on them, but he did feel that Dallas and its citizens should not be "throttled" in expressing their dislike of the United Nations.

Ironically, Dallas was engaged at the time in a promotional program inviting the world to visit it. Brochures printed in German, French, English and Spanish were being distributed in fifty-one major cities through Air

France's world-wide offices. They told of Dallas, a jet-age city with old-fashioned southwestern hospitality and charm.

At the same time—on UN Day itself—the fervor of the far right reached an extraordinary pitch. A handbill was distributed around town, dropped into automobiles and scattered over parking lots. It cast President Kennedy in the role of a wanted criminal. Under two photographs of the President—the classic full-face and profile shots of the fugitive poster—the copy read verbatim:

WANTED
FOR
TREASON

THIS MAN is wanted for treasonous activities against the United States:

1. Betraying the Constitution (which he swore to uphold):
   He is turning the sovereignty of the U.S. over to communist controlled United Nations.
   He is betraying our friends (Cuba, Katanga, Portugal) and befriending our enemies (Russia, Yugoslavia, Poland).
2. He has been WRONG on innumerable issues affecting the security of the U.S. (United Nations —Berlin wall—Missle [sic] removal—Cuba— Wheat deals—Test Ban Treaty, etc.)

3. He has been lax in enforcing Communist Regulation laws.
4. He has given support and encouragement to the Communist inspired racial riots.
5. He has illegally invaded a sovereign State with federal troops.
6. He has consistantly [*sic*] appointed Anti-Christians to Federal office: Upholds the Supreme Court in its Anti-Christian rulings. Aliens and known Communists abound in Federal offices.
7. He has been caught in fantastic LIES to the American people (including personal ones like his previous marraige [*sic*] and divorce).

11 | Preparing for the visit of John F. Kennedy

The controversy at the Museum of Fine Arts did not excite the leadership of Dallas very much. The general reaction was that the whole thing was a tempest in a teapot and should be settled and forgotten. Criticism of the city came principally from art columnists and from *Art News,* a magazine not part of the required reading of Citizens' Council members. The jostling of Lyndon

Johnson and his wife did raise some eyebrows and, as I said, may have cost the Republicans Texas. But, it did not cost them Dallas, where Alger, placard and all, was handily elected and where the city went strongly for Nixon and Lodge.

Some people did begin to worry seriously about their city's national reputation, but most did not. A good many practical businessmen were more worried about Johnson's own reaction to the incident than they were about national criticism of Dallas. The business leaders of the community are nothing if not realists, and when the Kennedy-Johnson ticket carried the country these leaders foresaw arid years ahead for Dallas. No American city in the twentieth century progresses very far without the interest and benevolence of Washington.

A couple of weeks after the election, I had lunch with a Dallas Democrat who said bitterly: "This town's in great shape now. We've got a congressman not even the Republicans talk to, we've got a Vice President who hates our guts and we've got a good, Irish Catholic politician in the White House who remembers where his votes came from—or didn't come from. Eight years of this and we'll be lucky if we're still bigger than Waco." Waco is a central Texas city, with a population of roughly 100,000.

But the Stevenson incident really shocked the city. Not only did the liberal press of the nation hop all over

Dallas, but one of the city's own newspapers, the *Dallas Times-Herald*, came out with a savage editorial that bore the simple headline "Dallas Disgrace." Written by A. C. Greene, the editorial impressed the rest of the country as being sensible self-rebuke, and it impressed the citizens of Dallas because after all these years of standing for home and motherhood, the *Times-Herald* had suddenly developed a bugle voice. More than the editorials, the disgusting incident itself hit hard at the conscience of the citizens. That this gentle and dignified man of high office should have been attacked in their city was horrifying to rational citizens, including most of the civic leaders. In scores of conversations after Stevenson was insulted, I heard men say, "This town has gone nuts. What on earth has happened to us?" Or, "What are we going to do about these idiots? They're going to have to add a line to the city limits sign, saying, CITY LIMITS OF DALLAS—UNSAFE!"

The men who have spent their lives trying to build a good city were badly jolted. Dallas depends enormously on its contacts with other cities throughout the United States. It is a transportation center and its airport is the fifth busiest in the nation. Its bankers, lawyers, insurance men, oil men and other businessmen do business with New York, Los Angeles and other cities almost daily, and they themselves travel a great deal. They were unaccustomed to the feeling of shame rather than pride when they signed "Dallas" to a hotel register, and to doing their business in New York while even a Republican newspaper like the *New York Herald Tribune* was condemning their city.

"I think," Stanley Marcus said one day to a group of his officers, "that we ought to see whether or not we can persuade President Kennedy to change his mind about visiting Dallas. Frankly, I don't think this city is safe for it."

The meeting in Mr. Marcus's office, crowded with pictures, pieces of sculpture and artifacts from all over the world, went on for three hours. I remember thinking how often the officers had met in it to discuss matters involving not only the store, but the city itself. There, this stocky, intelligent man, a part of everything that happened in Dallas, would tell us of new plans for the city. He would discuss educational or artistic endeavors which he thought the store as a corporation should back. The atmosphere in these meetings was always one of progress, of doing new things to better the city.

Suddenly now the officers were gathered together to discuss whether or not to un-invite a President of the United States to this same city. No one was thinking in terms of assassination. They were all thinking of spitting and striking and throwing things and the kind of indignities they had seen before. They were thinking of the President himself being harmed or insulted. They were thinking in terms of how Dallas might best avoid another scandalous incident so soon after the last one.

Mr. Marcus's meeting was not the only expression of concern. Ambassador Stevenson telephoned Arthur Schlesinger, Jr., to suggest that the President cancel his visit to Dallas. Stevenson had promised Jack Goren, the United Nations Day Chairman, that he would do so. In a limousine going to the airport Goren had suggested that Stevenson talk to the President about the right-wing fanatics in the city and warn him that a trip to Dallas might not be safe.

Stevenson agreed, and he called Schlesinger. But a day or two later he reconsidered and called Schlesinger again to say that if the President felt his trip to be politically feasible, he should go ahead and make it. I am sure that Ambassador Stevenson, like many others, was counting on the secret service to protect the President in case the Dallas police could not.

Many of the city's leaders met at lunch for a discussion of this same problem. The consensus everywhere came down to two major points:

1. You simply cannot un-invite a President of the United States to your city.

2. If you did, the President, especially a man like Kennedy, would not pay the slightest attention.

It was decided, therefore, that the President was going to come, whatever warnings he might receive, and that it was up to the city to organize a campaign which would keep the mouth of the far right closed, at least during the President's stay. The campaign was organized in very much the same way that peaceful integration was arranged. Sam Bloom, the advertising man, was put in charge of it. The Citizens' Council agreed to serve as the host organization for a luncheon at the Trade Mart where Kennedy was to make his talk. The preparations were as usual: the mayor was asked to make a statement imploring his people to greet the President with warmth and hospitality and not to show disapproval to any of his policies by actions disrespectful of his office. The newspapers agreed to cooperate fully in the campaign. The police force was alerted to spot any agitator quickly and to remove him before trouble could start. Unfriendly pickets were discouraged, but if any showed up they were to be placed well back in the crowd, away from Kennedy's person. The preachers were encouraged to advise their congregations to turn out in a friendly spirit.

But this time The Establishment was not the sole director of the campaign. It had to contend with White House planning as well.

"It was a mess from hell to breakfast," Sam Bloom said, "and I suppose these things will always be. We were plugging along at the agency, trying to get organized for the visit, when a guy comes in and says, 'Well,

Mr. Bloom, I want you to know that I am the coordinator for the White House.' I said, 'Well, how do you do?'
And he left. The next day I had a call from a man up
in Washington who said, 'Good morning, Mr. Bloom.
I'm the coordinator for the White House.' 'Well, we
seem to have two coordinators for the White House,' I
said, 'because somebody came in to see me yesterday
and said *he* was the coordinator for the White House.'
Well, this guy in Washington said, 'Don't bother about
him; my authority supercedes his.' I said, 'Okay, fine.'
The next day we had a call from another man up there
and he said, 'Good morning, Mr. Bloom. I'm the coordinator for the White House,' and I said, 'Well, as far as I
can see, you fellows better start coordinating because
you're the third coordinator and it seems to me that
what you ought to be doing is coordinating the coordinators.'

"Then we had the Yarborough interests, the Kennedy
interests, the Johnson interests, the Connally interests,
some labor leaders, some loyal democrats, some non-
loyal democrats, all plugging at us for tickets and we
didn't have enough. Somebody told us that the White
House itself wanted 150 tickets and Governor Connally
would need fifty. We marked the White House tickets
'W.H.' and the Connally tickets 'G.C.' Before it was all
over we had to get them back because we figured these
would just be handed out at random, and we were get-

ting too many protests from the people who couldn't get in.

"It was the White House that wanted the motorcade. Actually, in Washington, they kept telling us we were trying to tighten things up too much. Maybe we were, but we were worried because of the Johnson and the Stevenson incidents. We didn't want anything to happen. They kept telling us that Kennedy handled these things very well, that he had seen lots of pickets and that they didn't bother him. So they ordered the motorcade. They wanted to make him visible to the maximum number of people over the maximum number of miles within the time scheme. We got the idea that we were a lot more nervous than anybody else about the reception the President would get. We were thinking that incidents that might not be important somewhere else would make news if they happened in Dallas.

"I want to say one nice thing about the security people, the secret service. They were the best people we dealt with. They knew what they wanted, they put it on lists and all we had to do was to provide it at the right time, which of course we did.

"I'd also like to say that I think the campaign worked very well. Dallas was well prepared by the various media for the President's visit and you could tell it if you were out there. After all, there were a couple of hundred thousand people, all friendly and all waving and smiling. In spite of all the earlier confusion, I think the presentation that had been planned was honorable, modest and decent. The speeches had been held to a minimum and Erik Jonsson was handling things fine."

As everyone knows, Mrs. John Connally, the wife of the governor of Texas, agreed with Mr. Bloom. "Well, you certainly can't say the people of Dallas are against you today," she said to President Kennedy only moments before he was shot and killed and her own husband seriously wounded.

"It was as though a limb fell on him," Holland Mc-Combs said.

In a phrase, I think he expressed the bewilderment of the citizens at Kennedy's apparently having been assassinated in Dallas by a Marxist. The first thought in the minds of the scores of people I've seen since the assassination was that it must have been done by a member of the right wing. Many of the local rightists themselves thought so. I watched the color go completely from a man's face at the Imperial Club when the murder was announced. Politically, he stands well to the right of Goldwater. At that moment, he was convinced that one of his colleagues had committed murder. We may never know all the facts about the assassination of President

John F. Kennedy, but if this lonely Marxist outcast did indeed commit murder in Dallas, history has a bitter irony.

The President was shot at 12:20 P.M. on Friday, November 22. From that moment, life became a nightmare for many people living in Dallas. It was unthinkable that the President had been shot. It was unbearable that he had been shot in Dallas.

Even the sorrow had scarcely penetrated when the press began to arrive. They came in droves, on airplanes, in cars—one *Life* photographer sat on the arm of my wife's seat on an American Airlines plane from California. They swarmed in, taking over the hotels and restaurants, deluging anyone they could find with questions.

For the citizen of Dallas, the phone at home kept ringing. On November 23 I answered nineteen long distance calls from all over the United States and one from London. Most people were trying to say that we of Dallas should not take personal responsibility, that it could have happened anywhere. On Sunday, after Oswald's death, most of the same people called back wondering whether Dallas had lost its sanity. Some leading Dallas citizens went on television to proclaim that what had happened was not the city's fault. Quickly they were laying the predicate for a type of defense heard often later: It was the act of a lone lunatic, and lunatics are anywhere, not just in Dallas.

Then a minister named Bill Holmes, of the Northaven Methodist Church, got into his pulpit on Sunday morning and delivered a blistering sermon in which he claimed that some Dallas children had applauded the death of the President. His statements were picked up by CBS on Walter Cronkite's program, and Holmes had to go into seclusion to get away from threats of violence.

The public relations apparatus went into effect quickly. Everyone was to cooperate with the press and try to obtain the best possible face for the city. By Sunday, the city gave the appearance of having a worldwide press convention. The correspondents from abroad had arrived. They came from England, from France, from the Netherlands, from Germany, from Scandinavia, from South America, and they started writing stories explaining the city after they had been here for three hours.

Many Dallas people, with the great love they have for their city and state, lived for days with tears welling in their eyes and sometimes streaming down their cheeks. Some of the reporters, making points, made mincemeat of these men. A friend of mine challenged one of the reporters to a fight, having been baited all evening to this point, having fallen for the bait and having made the reporter's point for him: Texans are belligerent. The pressure on the newspapers, on the police, on the FBI and on the civic leaders was close to unbearable. Erik Jonsson, for example, who had chaired the luncheon at which Kennedy was to speak, said the four days were "the most unbelievable experience of my life." For Jonsson and for many others, it was like standing in the middle of a huge room, in the midst of a horde of faceless enemies, swirling about and striking, again and again, without reason. I remember the sad words of one man who asked, "What on earth did we ever do to deserve this?"

Activities stopped. The opera performance was called off; the charity ball was cancelled. Restaurants and stores closed, as did most of the offices in the city.

By Tuesday, when most of the stores had reopened, everything had turned into a detective story. There were almost as many theories as there were people, and in the theory department, the French journalists were the champions. It was a right-wing plot, it was a Castro plot, it was a Mafia plot, it had something to do with sex, and so on. The theories were ingenious and one or another of them may even be right, for all I know. I remember, though, that during one evening when the possibilities were discussed endlessly into the night, a woman I know suddenly remembered the subject of this detective story and began to cry.

For a while, Dallas was like a bombed city—numb, disbelieving, going through the motions.

And not very many motions, at that. Everything was closed on Monday, and for a long time the Imperial Club, Dallas Club, the City Club and all the other luncheon places in Dallas seemed quiet and strained. The electric selling push that is such a trademark of the city, that you can see and feel on the streets, was gone, and I think some hate that had not been there before came into the city. I know I felt it when I heard a man say that he was getting "God damned sick and tired of all that publicity for Jackie Kennedy on television." I remember that I hated him.

All over America, I suppose, nerves were raw and tears were close, but in Dallas, in addition to all that, there was that damned bass drum beating into our senses: "Dallas, it was Dallas. . . . Dallas, it was Dallas. . . . Dallas, it was Dallas. . . ."

12 | After the tragedies

In the weeks that followed the assassination, the city began little by little to settle back into its normal patterns.
The Dallas Cowboys' football games went on as scheduled, the opera put on its delayed performance, the symphony went back to work and the atmosphere of bustle
and potential achievement returned to Dallas.

A Dallas woman named Eleanor Cowan wrote a letter to *Time* magazine in which she questioned the innocence of the city in the events of the tragic four days. Newspapers immediately announced that she had been suspended as a teacher in the Dallas public school system. A cry was raised and Mrs. Cowan became—for a while—a *cause célèbre*. The clergy and others went to her defense, and it developed that she may not, after all, have been suspended. Instead, Superintendent W. T. White of the Dallas public school system had written her a note asking her to come in and see him about the "judgment" involved in writing the letter. Mrs. Cowan missed classes for a couple of days and then returned to school. The suddenly aroused liberals of the city promised to keep a watchful eye on Mrs. Cowan to be sure that she would be engaged again for next year.

Among the ministers there was a great deal of breast-beating. One after another, they deplored what had happened and berated the climate of a community in which such things could occur. Some members of their congregations were moved and thoughtful, but others were enraged. A common complaint was "How can you blame a whole city for the acts of one lunatic?" This, of course, is not what the preachers were trying to say, but it was a quick, easy way not to answer what they did say. A more acute criticism came from some of the people who actually agreed with the preachers that the citizens needed to reassess themselves.

These people asked: "That's all very fine, now, but tell me where the preachers were when all of this was building up? How many did we hear from before the assassination? Not very many."

Dallas is a church-going city. It has the largest Baptist church in the world, the largest Methodist church in the world, one of the largest Presbyterian churches in the world, a very important Church of Christ, strong Roman Catholic churches and immense synagogues, both Orthodox and Reform. Altogether there may be 800 churches in the city.

Not long ago, the Reverend Luther Holcombe, a liberal Baptist who is head of the Council of Churches, said: "It is the small ones [churches] that give me hope . . . to me, it is encouraging to look at these tiny churches all through the city where the preacher can't count on much money to build a new room, but he can call for some carpenters and their wives who can make coffee. There's a real sincerity of religious conviction in Dallas. This touches me and gives me hope."

For the first of the year, Mr. Stanley Marcus wrote his widely quoted advertisement, "What's Right with Dallas," in which he called for an end to absolutism and pointed out some of the things Dallas had not done, such as improve its slum situation. To his gratification, the number of crackpot and critical letters he received was far outweighed by a virtual avalanche of favorable comment.

As the New Year began, The Establishment of the city continued for the most part to go about business as usual, but there were still a few who were looking deeply into themselves and their colleagues and into the structure of the whole city, wondering what had gone wrong and what could be done to make it right.

In February Melvin Belli, chief counsel for Jack Ruby, subpoenaed 170 leaders of Dallas. Mr. Belli was trying to show before Judge Joe Brown that it would be impossible for Ruby to get a fair trial in Dallas. In the meantime, Sam Bloom, the advertising man, was catching brickbats for having volunteered his services as public relations advisor to the Judge. This being one of the few times in American judicial history when a criminal court judge has been represented by a public relations agency, the press had a field day, which was exactly what Bloom expected.

"There are forty press seats in that court room," he explained to me. "Between three and five hundred reporters were planning to come. No telegraph wires are set up, the phones are inadequate, and just plain physically, some of the reporters wouldn't have a snowball's chance in hell of getting a story out of Dallas. All we did was help set up the physical machinery. We haven't written a single release and we haven't told the judge what to do and what not to do." Judge Brown barred the television cameras from his court. To most observers it does not seem unlikely that he had strong advice on this point.

In the matter of winning a change of venue for Ruby's trial, Belli's method was simply to put Dallas itself on trial. His argument was that the city already felt itself to be on trial and that nothing but a death penalty against Ruby could clear its name. This put the witnesses in the position of stating that they thought that Belli was right, and that the city was on trial; or that the city was not on trial, which would mean that it considered itself totally innocent of these matters.

The leaders of Dallas themselves had a different point of view, but it tied in with Belli's point. They too wanted the trial moved, simply because out of some 400 reporters, 360 would be sitting in Dallas, Texas, unable even to attend the trial they had come to cover. In the eyes of these reporters, Dallas seemed unlikely to be able to do anything right. Sensibly enough, the leaders would have preferred these reporters to twiddle their thumbs in irritation and frustration somewhere other than Dallas.

With motives so mixed, the testimony was naturally divided between those who thought Ruby could get as fair a trial in Dallas as anywhere else (implying that he would not be able to get a fair trial anywhere), and those who stated that Dallas was too emotionally involved in clearing its own name to be fair to a man whose life was at stake.

Belli, of course, in keeping with his campaign for a change of venue, held the latter opinion. But the leaders of Dallas wondered what would happen if the trial was not held in the city where the crime occurred. Melvin Belli could have tried the case in Tanganyika and received full publicity value for it. But the city of Dallas would have been denied the chance to try an accused criminal from within its own borders.

Meantime, Mrs. Marina Oswald made a dignified appearance on television in an interview with Eddie Barker of CBS, during which she said, at last, that she believed her husband had killed President Kennedy.

Oswald's mother kept protesting that the secret service was not allowing her to see her daughter-in-law, but no one had the impression that her daughter-in-law was particularly troubled about it. *Life* magazine paid Mrs. Oswald, Sr., a token fee which developed out of a long and exclusive interview that one of its reporters got with Mrs. Oswald after the assassination. Talk of money floated through the cool Texas air. Mrs. Tippit's fund went over six hundred thousand dollars in donations, and thus complicated forever what had been a simple life. Marina Oswald was to write a book, and Jack Ruby was to write a book, but in Ruby's case Melvin Belli had first crack at any royalties as a guarantee against his fee.

Money and publicity lent their venal presence to the atmosphere of Dallas in the winter of 1963-64. It was not, on the whole, a climate to give substance to mankind's higher aspirations.

But then, man has always mixed in his heroism with his greed, and it is unlikely that human nature will suddenly change during the trial of a night club operator in Dallas. We will go on, all of us, doing an occasional large thing well, and a million little things badly. We will rise to a height now and again and then fall back into our petty natures until the time comes when something forces us, always at the last possible moment, to rise up again.

As I review these pages concerning what I have noted during seventeen years in Dallas, Texas, I am reminded of a story Holland McCombs told me just after the assassination. One of the foreign magazines hired an American writer-photographer to do a thorough exposé on Dallas. At the time, this was quite usual. People throughout the world were shocked at what had happened in the city and were quite ready to read anything which attacked it. This reporter, however, was a responsible, thinking man. After a day of exploration, he walked up Elm Street with McCombs.

"He kicked an old, left-over half-pint into an alley and looked at a fat man standing in the sun outside his pawn shop," McCombs told me. "Back further, you could see the Republic [Bank Building] and the other big buildings. 'Hell, Holland,' he said. 'What's so damn different?' "

Dallas seems to me not so "damn different." If there are local factors which are special to it, there are other factors special to other communities. The major problems of Dallas are common to many American cities, and if some of these problems are more pressing in Dallas than they are elsewhere, some of its virtues are equally distinctive.

One night a year or so ago, a young woman, recently arrived from the east, sat down and tore the city apart. She attacked its culture, its materialism, its crime rate, its political atmosphere, its newspapers, its anti-intellectualism and the fact that you can't get a drink after midnight. She covered it all in what I thought was a fine piece of invective. But a male guest spoke up. I am paraphrasing him, but I do not think he will mind.

"To begin with," he said, "you speak of 'it.' Who is 'it'? 'It' is people, and I know these people better than you do. If they are non-musical, they are not anti-musical. If they are non-intellectual, they are not anti-intellectual. If they are materialistic, so am I; I am simply not so good at it as they are. If they are fearful, so am I fearful, and if they are insecure, I am, too. If they are certain they are right politically, perhaps they have not been proved wrong as often as I have. If they are violent, I have seen much worse; and if they are emotional, I would prefer that to cold cruelty. If its newspapers speak with one voice, then you and I can speak with the other, and if we do not, it is only because these people you attack may not love us; we are as vulnerable, then, as they.

"I know them better than you. They made me welcome, as different from them as I am. I can never be identical with them, but I have not been cast out by them. There is always a meeting ground; not yours or mine, but they will move further to establish it than you have. For me—I will move a long way."

Some kind of counter-attack on the young lady was to be expected. This one impressed and moved me because it came from the first 'cellist of the Dallas Symphony Orchestra, a Latvian by birth. His name is Lev Aronson, he spent six years in German concentration camps and he is Jewish. He spoke very little English when he came to Dallas in 1945, but it is his home now, and this is what he had to say about it.

For me, his was a good description of the things I,

too, have liked. Some people talk about the limitless Texas sky, which gives a man the impression that anything is possible. Erik Jonsson talks of helpfulness. The Brooklyn-born mayor says, "A lot of places, you are on your own; they don't give a damn about you. Down here, they really try to help you. I think they do."

There are many things about Dallas to like and respect. But it is a disturbed city in a disturbed nation, and the reasons for these disturbances will not vanish overnight.

"Where the hell is Cambodia?" Sam Bloom says. "People see a headline, and suddenly we're in trouble in Cambodia. It's got to be somebody's fault, so we start attacking somebody. The news is too fast and too confusing. We see a headline and we go over to the atlas to find out where Cambodia is. Then we attack somebody about it. We do more damn talking about things we don't know anything about than anybody in history."

The profusion of events *is* particularly difficult in a democracy, where everybody knows immediately what has happened; not why, just what. The newspapers, the radio and television commentators also do not know why a good deal of the time; nevertheless, they tell us what. It's all too much. The rent has to be paid, and the girls have to be educated, and the eleven-year-old is having Spanish trouble, and, according to *Time* magazine, the seventeen-year-old is probably pregnant; Cambodia is too much.

So are a lot of other things for Americans in the midst of the twentieth century. The Negro's extraordinary march has been hard to bear, both for Negroes and for whites. Those whites who fight it are mixed. Some are hopeless bigots, some are profit-makers and many more are confused and fearful because the order is changing and all the values they were taught have suddenly crumpled. Any change frightens most people, and big change frightens them more.

But there are other white people, who argue for the Negroes and are yet filled with both doubt and guilt— doubt because they are not confident of their own feelings, guilt because they doubt. And there are millions more who feel guilt because they don't care enough. They feel they should, but it would be easier if the whole thing would go away.

Finally, there are some who feel strongly and honestly, but who know that it will take years, long beyond their time, and that this heavy burden of negotiation, disappointment, flaring violence, cajoling, imploring, attack and defense will be upon them for the rest of their lives. And the Negroes, if a white man can judge it, must get a deep joy when they sing their song, "We Shall Overcome," and a deep sadness when they know that they will be singing it and singing it and singing it. . . .

Some of the civil rights question has nothing to do with hatred but only with the trend of Americans to move to the cities. In Cincinnati, 64,000 Negroes moved to the city over the course of a decade. In that time, the city had created 20,000 new jobs. Forty-four thousand Negroes either displaced other people or went jobless. It is a typical problem. Initially it has nothing to do with hatred, but it can cause hatred. Dallas achieved its first integration without incident after a skillfully organized campaign and because its Negro population is about 15 per cent of its total, not 50 per cent or more. Still, the Negroes will come to Dallas and Houston and the other big cities of Texas and they will have to be absorbed. It is in Texas, as elsewhere, a long, long road.

13 | Epilogue

I am, as this is written, thirty-six years old. When I was eleven, a Puerto Rican boy held up two of us in New York City between Madison and Fifth Avenues on Ninety-sixth Street. Both of us attended St. Bernard's School, and we wore caps with a school shield on them. He held us up with a pen knife, and he was smaller than either of us. We simply separated; whichever way he moved, one of us had him. He looked at us, and then he began to run. I have not seen in Dallas or anywhere a look of deeper hatred than the look on that small boy's face when he knew he didn't have a chance, knife or not. I remember the incident partly because the look on his face when he first thrust the knife at us was quite different—timid, almost asking us to let him get away with it.

That was twenty-five years ago in New York, but it was confusing to me then, and to my white friend, and certainly to the Puerto Rican boy. I remember thinking we should have let him have the money, all two dollars of it. And I remember thinking I was wrong; and I remember wondering whether it was right or wrong, a question which has stayed with me over this quarter-century. Other Americans have also wondered and, for many, bewilderment makes for absolutism.

Americans were told long ago what the American Dream was all about. So far as I know, this dream said only that in America people could rise from nothing to power and great riches. To various degrees, Texans have made this dream come true. Now they are told that it was a bad dream, that because they have made money they are probably un-American, that material success is a liability, not an asset. They were told what to do, they did it, and now they are told it wasn't worth doing. If they lash back, one can understand.

Yet in the end we do not live in the first confused age of man's history, and it is our responsibility to cope with our own confusion. Dallas, in the judgment of the world, has not met that responsibility. Perhaps nothing before now really compelled it to do so, but at this point it must. The eyes of the world are on it, and Dallas does business with the world.

John Kennedy will live in the minds of his countrymen because of the things he did, the things he tried to do, the things he might have done and the style with which he approached life. Memory of the assassination itself will fade quickly, as shock and pain always do, and Americans concern themselves with how the first Texas President handles himself.

In Dallas they have been talking about memorials. A committee has been organized and has received suggestions on how the city might best pay tribute to the man who was killed within its limits. They have decided on a memorial at the site of the assassination and a gift to the Kennedy memorial library at Harvard University in Cambridge, Massachusetts.

The people of Dallas might well recall President Kennedy's quest for excellence. When something was to be written, he wanted it written well; when the 'cello was played, he wanted the note precise and the piece well chosen; when a fullback cut through tackle, he wanted it to be a total effort, smartly and bruisingly done; when a man said something, he wanted it to make sense and to shed a new light. He cared for excellence and disliked the shoddy and the careless. If he could have his choice, I think he would wish his memorial in Dallas to be the pursuit of excellence in the city in which he died.

It is not impossible. Nothing in Dallas will change tomorrow, or even soon after that. But if the ingredients for success have been in its men, then the ingredients for excellence may be in them and in their sons. Next year the Dallas orchestra will play in Carnegie Hall, and it will have ninety musicians for the first time in its history. A fine scientific research center, specializing in faculty rather than buildings, is going up. The Citizens' Council is reassessing itself to see whether or not a business elite is the best ruling group, or whether the good minds of the city, unaccompanied by money, should be asked to supply a conscience to the cash.

Nothing has been solved in Dallas. Venal man continues to wrestle with his hero-structure, and more than half the time the dwarf wins out. But one step is taken here, another there. In his lifetime, Kennedy used to quote to the secret service men who accompanied him some famous lines by Robert Frost:

The woods are lovely, dark and deep,
But I have promises to keep;
And miles to go before I sleep,
And miles to go before I sleep.

By the time these miles have been traveled in Dallas, no one will remember that Kennedy liked the poem, but in the accomplishments of the future someone with a memory may recall that part of the impetus for change and reassessment in Dallas was the shock and horror of this man's death and the dreary things which led up to it.

A few weeks ago, I left Dallas for New York on a Braniff flight. The stewardess made her usual speech, and at the end of it she told us we would be landing at John F. Kennedy Airport at 9:30 P.M. A couple of hours later the captain's voice came over the loud-speaker and told us that we would be landing a little early at Idlewild Airport.

I remember feeling sadness. But just before our arrival the stewardess asked us to fasten our seat belts. "We are making our approach now to John F. Kennedy Airport in New York," she said.

Coming up from Dallas, some of us felt better.

Index

*The text is set in Linotype Caledonia, one of W. A. Dwiggins'
many contributions to typographical design. Caledonia was cut
by Linotype in 1939.*

*The display face used on the chapter openings and on the title
page is Consort condensed. The Consort series was developed in
England in 1956 after a Victorian Egyptian design by the Ste-
phenson, Blake Letter Foundry, a foundry which can be traced
back to the late 15th century.*

*The book is printed by letterpress on Warren's 66 text paper,
with composition, printing and binding by H. Wolff Book Manufacturing Co., New York.*

Design: Adrianne Onderdonk